AF235145

Albert Bright

AstronEfficiencyOnomy Solutions

The formulas of astronomy as a solution for greater efficiency

Volume 3 of GlobalOnomy

© 2019 Albert Bright
1st German edition: 2019
© 2021 Albert Bright
1st British edition – as 3/3 trilogy of GlobalOnomy, 2021

AstronEfficiencyOnomy

ISBN Paperback: 9783753482514

9 783753 482514

Editor: www.world-wide-wealth.com
Author: Albert Bright
Envelope design, illustration: Albert Bright
Proofreading: www.world-wide-wealth.com

Translation: www.world-wide-wealth.com

Printing and Publishing: BoD - Books on Demand,
Norderstedt / Germany

This book arose from the fascination of the universe with its seemingly limitless dimensions and growth - and the idea of using its laws of nature as a recipe for a better world.

Albert Bright

Astronomy-rules for a better GlobalOnomy: economy & currency, knowledge & wisdom, peace & liberty, health & wealth as well as welfare & sustainability - world-wide!

.

Outline

A. INTRODUCTION

Idea. If you search for "idea" on the Internet – and then look at the "pictures" about it, then mostly glowing glow-bulbs appear. Second abundance are rays, third are lightnings, fourth are thought clouds/bubbles, fifth heads and sixth brains. According to the pictures on the Internet, ideas seem to have a lot to do with energy and space. But also with lighting (recognizing something) or epiphany (a light, as sudden idea in the brain). Many images also show processes (if-then-relationships). And hereby often time aspects (processes in the time sequence). The latter is synonymous with a delay in the aspects after an idea: Vision, mission, goal, target, realization. One would very much like to have all at the moment of the emergence of ideas. And with enough free space to enjoy immediately.

Universe grows faster, than humanity can (could) calculate with the formulas at the actual status-quo. Are there (hidden) formulas, which work with more efficiency, than we are used to think of in our models?
To get things quicker, immediately? There are. We found some.

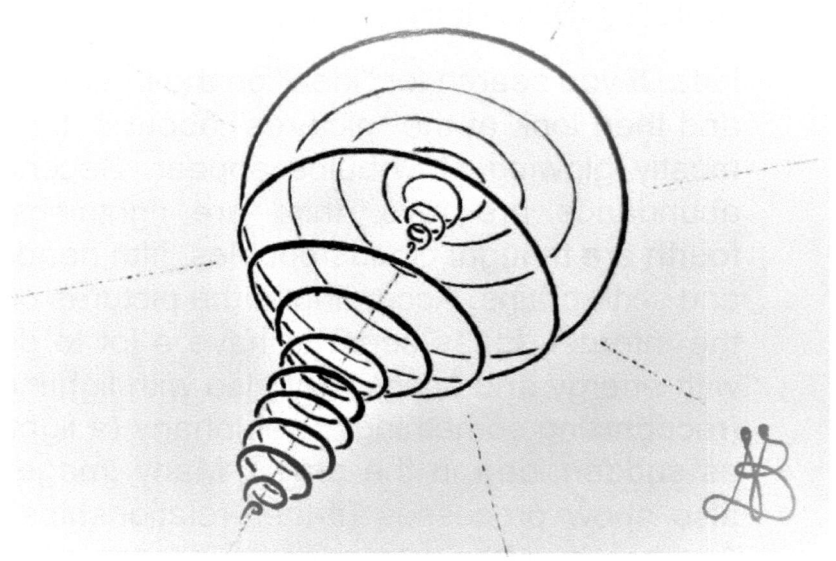

An idea, a glow-bulb, indeed illuminates a previously dark area. But the ideas frame is very fragile - made of glass. And each idea was fed in a previously dark area, with "unknown" forces. And apparently these forces as well can interrupt this energy supply at any time.

Quanta appear and disappear here and there as well in universe. Like ideas in our brain.

As well our environment has the power to do so - everything can stay the same, as before, at any time. At least in the corresponding "environment", like a "controlled" area. The Earth is flat – and the center of the universe. Basta. Galileo-Galilei glow-bulb-glass destroyed. Energy supply stopped via excommunication. No one should be able to think about, nor see reality.

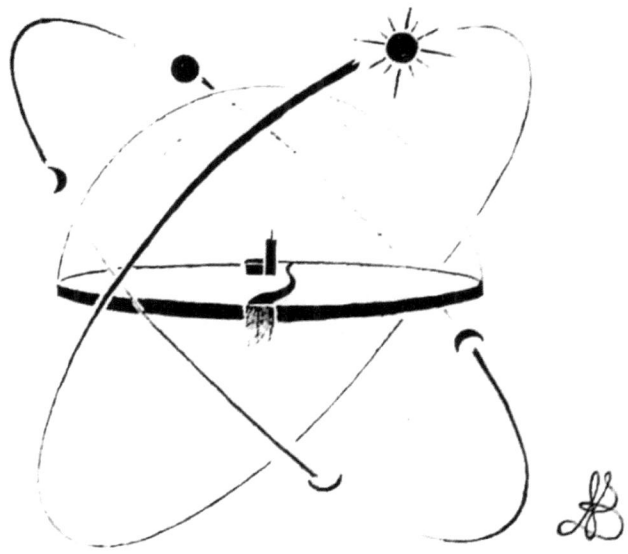

"Enlightenments" should be purely the believe in Good and Church. "Faith" can displace "reality". Unfortunately, far too often.

Everything around this thought construction remains dark, at least for those who sit in that hypothetical construct.

But the rest of the universe is growing. Ever further, ever bigger,…

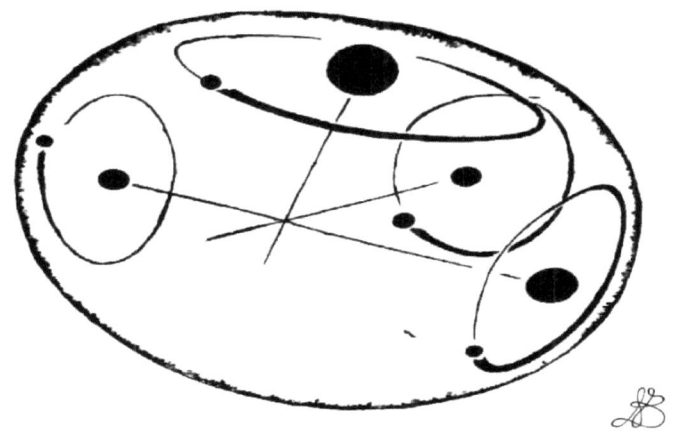

…always more beautiful, and better, for all.

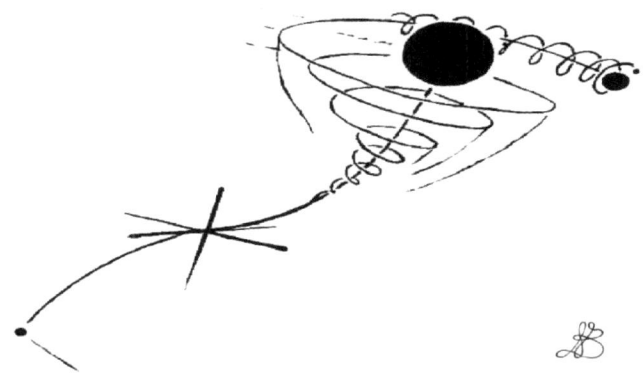

Not only for a small number of self-appointed rulers.

What is unfortunately not shown in the Internet images is the benefit of an idea. Although almost every idea may be an increase in efficiency.

And so, the simplism (on the Internet) of our first two great researches continues:

1)   We investigated the "time" – and found as images on the Internet primarily "clocks".

2)   We examined the "space" and found on the Internet primarily "chambers" as pictures.

3)   In "ideas" we now find primarily "light-bulbs".

With our formulas for TIME [01] and SPACE [02] in the last two books we showed what is possible if different perspectives and new thoughts are considered and followed up. With ideas that can increase EFFICIENCY, even more is achievable, as we want to show in this book.

According to our formulas, this is also the case in the universe. The central objective of universe - in the course of time - seems to be "efficiency". And looking deeper at this efficiency, since the existence of universe, the primary targets seem to be: "space" and "energy". We should therefore focus this much more on Earth in order to be as efficient as the universe in the course of time.

Ideas are what distinguishes mankind. And what can advance knowledge, wisdom, efficiency, prosperity, peace and freedom. At least, if the environment is "harmonious". And or there is enough "power" i.e. "energy". Energy in astronomy means the "power to do work" and is needed to achieve "results". As in universe, so on our earth. The most popular pictures of power are: energy, pull and push. But there are far more powers, which may lead to many top ideas.
And knowledge, resulting from earlier ideas, is the basis of new ideas. Knowledge is the only raw material that increases when used. If we invested much more in the education of all humanity, the basis for global efficiency-gains, wisdom, ingenuity and thus prosperity would be many times better. Not only

because many more new ideas would be created. But also, because many more people would then understand that the fanaticism or/and the greed for power of some "leaders" does not lead to prosperity. Most of the "you must believe" or "you must follow" lead to misallocations. They lead to the destruction of prosperity and environmental resources for wrong purposes. The "space" (liberty) as such, for everyone to have own ideas and to follow his own way (orbit) is one of the top efficiency-aspects, which universe does better than mankind.

There are nice solutions for prosperity in the book "AstronTimeOnomy" [01] and for freedom and peace solutions proposed in the book "AstronSpaceOnomy".[02] They should be implemented. Then all those inefficiencies resulting from self-centralization-focused, destructive and "gravity"-pushing, power-hungry, domineering "leaders", would no longer have a chance to persist. Democracy at the highest level would be possible. And world-wide-wealth achievable.

Politicians would have to have a very high level of education, wisdom, empathy, and transcendence to make their mark. And only those who have really good solutions for the entire population would have a chance of being elected. Wars? No rich and intelligent person goes to war. Especially if the (resistance) amount of intelligent people is large enough. Peace and freedom would also be achieved far easier than in todays´ constellations. And sustainability would no longer only be a catchword.

Unfortunately, humanity is currently focused on material aspects rather than the intellectual. Lamentably many people cannot afford the "intellectual" way in terms of time and money.

Thus, bubbles will continue to be built. And lots of "holes". Because a hole is the only phenomenon that gets bigger the more you take out. And the bigger, the greater the possible damage. Bubble-building speculators count with this. And turne away, to new bubbles, after having been "helped". There is obviously something wrong here. But material or visual greatness seems to matter to humans. "Too big to fail" often honored the "worst" in the cash flow crisis. And deprived the "normal" from a financial basis. And even allows a "keep it up" by means of hiding central aspects. These are bad-banks-"games", obligatory zero-interest-rates, endless debt, money-printing in breathtaking volumes - and speculative bubbles in unprecedented dimensions. And un-fortunately, all these aspects, with un-precedented in-efficiencies! Lamentably more and more other ("marginal") areas are falling into these "holes". Insurances, due to low interest rates; normal-size-companies due to the limited lending of banks, ...).

The same applies to holes in raw material mines, which need to be dredged faster and more "efficiently" because no one has (enough) money for sustainability. Only "cheap" is payable, desired, and bought. And the new financial "holes", that are needed to "repair" our "perforated" environment aren´t hardly to be financed - not even with the current "manipulated" capital market "rules".

We have a new economic model and a new currency model that can regulate better and finance everything. It is presented in the first book, "AstronTimeOnomy" [01]

And we have presented in a second book, "AstronSpaceOnomy" [02] a new sociology model, which can promote knowledge, freedom and peace - instead of materialistic short-sight-focus.

In the current book, "AstronEfficiencyOnomy" we now want to show some correlations. Synergies, of and with those formulas of TIME[03] and SPACE[03] presented in the first two books. On this basis, we want to show, that the universe is EFFICIENT – and leans towards SUSTAINABILITY. And on the basis of these findings, we give clues for greater efficiency and sustainability for humanity.

The variable(!)[04] SPACE is at the heart of our curiosity. And just as (energetic) ideas develop human beings, so the (energetic) SPACE seems to have a central role in the "development" of the universe. But: The brains people who learn a lot do not expand spatially. The same is valid for the apparent expansion of the universe. It mainly just seems to have (only) spatial increase. What we see (only) as space seems – at least according to our findings – to be more or something else, than (only) a 3-D dimension expansion.

SPACE also seems to be a kind of energy! Thus, SPACE in the universe would be comparable to the "energy" of "ideas", which we find as symbols when we search the internet for the word "idea": light-bulb-energy! Light moments! Mind flashes!

In this book we will also research what formulas and correlations the universe uses to develop. And then we will draw conclusions from these formulas. What can humanity improve, in order to develop itself and the world better.

With the previous ideas about SPACE (in AstronSpaceOnomy) we were able to decipher the 23% of "dark matter". And with the SPACE and TIME analyses of the present book, we are now able, to also decipher the previously unknown 72% of "dark energy". This now seems as bright to us, as a "path" to greater efficiency, knowledge, intelligence, empathy, wisdom, freedom, peace, transcendency and sustainability on our planet. On the basis of astronomy-rules.

Today we are pleased to present to you another book that provides more light to the interrelationships within universe. And we use its laws to illuminate optimizations across all borders on our Earth.

B. GENERAL

Einstein, after finalizing the "Simple Relativity Theory" started analyzing the sub-forces (especially gravity) of matter, within the "m" more deeply. This finally led to his "General Relativity Theory". Therefore, we felt encouraged to do it similar, but with the sub-forces of the "c" of its "Simple Relativity" formula. We did it, even if the "c" at Einstein is (was…) meant to be a constant(!) that has resulted from many experiments. And should not be interpreted as "light speed". Additionally, this (light-speed) constant at Einstein is (was…) under the "protection" of the ^{2}-square of the "c". The latter defines such an approach (according to status-quo astronomers) as "nonsense" because the speed of light is already the fastest possible speed. Increasing this speed on top by the power of 2 "doesn't make sense at all". It is unrealistic. It is not "visible" in the real universe. But we were able to prove invisible correlations. That "not-visible" has now become a "reasonable insight".

Matter, gravity and centrifugal force had already been analyzed by many researchers with different approaches. We therefore did not have much "field" left, to discover something really new. But by lateral- / cross-thinking and ignoring "prohibitions" we discovered the TIME and SPACE formulas. And as well their correlations with each other. And on top their correlations with other dimensions.

If, in the course of history, individual people had not gone forbidden paths time and again, then we would still be convinced, that the Earth is flat, the center of the universe – and all the stars orbit around us.

C. BOOSTER

Ever believed in an idea of someone else? Of course! The younger, the more likely you are to be inspired and engaged for something. Getting older, many people become sluggish and often don't want anything new. [05]

Ever had an own top idea? Of course! You will have experienced this feeling of suddenly having a solution for something that has occupied you for a long time. Suddenly, after jogging or/and showering or in the middle of the night, the solution is there. Suddenly the fog is gone. You can "see" (think!) very clearly. Why didn't we get to it before? You clap the flat palm of your hand to your head. And suddenly the heart starts pumping. And in the stomach, there is a feeling of happiness, as with the first love. It gets quite warm and a bit dizzy. You want to sit down or lie down on the beach or on the bench and just look at the sky. And then the head starts again with additional messages. What can you do with it?! Now there are further thoughts on what else is connected with it. Now you should start writing down quickly, otherwise many ideas and lateral thoughts are gone. What was the original idea, again? You're frightened. Can't be true! Was just there.

Ah, yes! Now I've got it again. Quickly write down in order. As writing with the right, my left hand automatically lifts. As if the body realizes that the right can't write as fast as the ideas come. And asks with the left hand for a little less pace. The hand writes almost automatically. Because the brain is already at a further point. Doodle. Hopefully I will be able to read my handwriting later. Hopefully I will know later what I meant by some abbreviations and keywords. Quickly create a drawing to make the connection clearer. I am deeply moved. Don't see what's happening around me. I'm not interested either. I just write. Now and here. I have to do it. Otherwise everything is gone. And then, after about half an hour – or was it three hours? – the thoughts fade. I'm starting to think in circles. Old thoughts sometimes mix with new things. But a lot of things just keep coming back. Repetitions strengthen. However, I am still writing many things, because it may become even clearer from a different perspective. Or even something else opens up. But yes, I get a little bit tired. And yes, I feel like I'm kind of empty, like exhausted. As if I just had a marathon run behind me. And my mind and eyes open up a little bit to the environment again. As if I'm still looking for more thoughts or tranquility in the area. Don't know what. Doesn't matter. But nothing new is coming any more. Where am I? Oh yes, was walking. And now I'm sitting here on the lawn. And the head is empty. Drained.

Luckily, I wrote everything down! I fly it over quickly. Simply because I want to make sure again, what it was about. And that I wrote it down safely. I don't understand everything at the moment. But I know I will be able to understand it again later, if I sit down and re-think more intensively. And my head keeps emptying. I'm starting to relax and enjoy. I think I've come a long way ahead. And that's a very nice feeling.

And then there are the sobering experiences that every creative person has to experience. At least, if it continues to fight for its ideas, despite resistance:

1. No one is interested;
2. The idea is ridiculed;
3. The idea is ignored;
4. The idea is opposed; and, if you are right,
5. The idea is taken for granted…

… suddenly all contradictors have always thought that way …

Be aware! An idea is a driver only if it moves something. That something does not have to be the astronomical "c^2" from Einstein's simple relativity. It can also be the outdated know-how from the library's books. But for "moving" something, you need to fight for your ideas.

Without ideas, the "m" moves only a little. But according to Newton also matter tends to move. So, that's ok. Yes? No! Einstein, with his "c^2" found a multiplier for the "m" with tremendous forces. And we are topping that. Still enormous things can be accomplished.

But only if one fights for it, just as Einstein. Despite his genius inventions, he had to fight very much for his ideas. Against the former "established" status-quo and its preservers. [06]

What are the "driving forces" behind an idea? And those behind the will to push that idea forward? Can the universe possibly offer solutions for this as well? In any case, at least rudimentary. When looking at our "speed"-formula and analyzing deeper the "speed"-booster, you will gain quite good insights. And why should matter and energy in a person's brain function differently than matter and energy according to our discovered SPACE, TIME, and EFFICIENCY-"booster" formulas of the universe? The universe determines us, and not the other way around. In my opinion, medicine, and in particular brain research, can still benefit greatly from findings in astronomy. We will take up this issue again later.

Openness to new things begins in one's own mind. One must be "free" (free space, free time) and have a good basis in order to develop something new. And you have to open up a lot of "space", have a curious brain to learn in order to invent new things. You have to have a great knowledge base in order to be able to develop something new. Ignorance knows everything. Wisdom knows, to know little. And you need time to listen, to research and to learn many existing aspects. Then you will find contradictions and new solutions.

As "driven" as we live in today's society, it is difficult to establish new things via the "normal" "science institutions". But if we continue to "submit" to the "dictation" of the material, time, limited capital (at least for "normal" projects) and the status-quo of the "knowledge institutions" (universities and professors), then we will never become as efficient as the universe.

The "knowledge" outside the universities increases by 100% every 2 years due to courageous researchers. However, the professorships do not. Todays´ bottleneck of knowledge not yet "officially recognized", is many times greater than at the times when the Church prevented any other interpretation of its messages.

Humanity needs better "knowledge institutions" – or far more profs and universities, with far more time, and far more openminded people towards new aspects.

The lack in quality is so big, that a new institution "Einstein-Institute" was established in USA, to set new rules.

Fortunately, there are institutions, such as the Patent Office for "real" (lamentably mainly technical / material) inventions. As well there are other institutions for sound ideas (though with a little less significance than a patent).

But human beings urgently need a new system for the "verification" of ideas. Or/and a completely new system of coexistence or economics. And inventors (outside of the universities) need a basis for not needing to survive on an immediate success of their own ideas or innovations. Humanity needs solutions as within AstronTimeOnomy[o1]. Otherwise, many ideas and booster-effects will get lost due to the lack of "space", "time" and "basis".

Humanity is more and more time-driven. This, as we will show, is also due to the primary MATERIAL orientation. But the combination of (less) TIME- AND (more) SPACE-aspects is fundamental. Also for humans in order to be able to become more efficient. And in terms of an efficiency multiplier, SPACE plays a far greater role than TIME. Astronomy has been presenting this to us for 13.8 billion years.

Einstein's c^2-"constant" was for us the basis for an approach to a "dynamic" "efficiency multiplier" towards SPACE. And a huge breakthrough on our path of knowledge.

And Einstein's "redefined and repurposed" c^2 as an (now) "efficiency multiplier" now includes our SPACE and TIME formulas We will show later. And this efficient dynamic multiplier has a much greater effect on everything that happens in the universe, than those sectors that have been primarily explored so far: "matter" and "energy" (from this matter). The latter, however, explains only 4.6% of the energy of the universe. In Einstein's c^2 multiplier, however, further energy is (was) hidden. It is now added, as we will show. In the multiplier, which we have newly defined, the un-known 95% of the energy of the universe were hidden: "dark matter" (23%) and "dark energy" (75%).

But yes, even in the universe, the SPACE fights against TIME. ....

In the first two books we already presented efficiency gains for humanity and our world through TIME and SPACE aspects. Now, this book will be about efficiency gains resulting from the extrapolation and the combination of SPACE and TIME.

In the beginning, we were thrilled to be able to interpret Einstein's c^2 as speed: We were able to prove with other physics formulas that speed can also be interpreted behind the c^2. We were able to invent the formulas for SPACE and TIME out of i.a. the standard km/h-speed-thoughts. And we could prove them to be plausible. That strengthened our enthusiasm.

But as thinking deeper progressed, we found that SPACE and TIME have much more to do with ENERGY and MATTER than with the spatial (3-D) room dimensions. Or with our time-in-a-watch- thoughts. Old-fashioned picture-results, which can be found as images when searching for SPACE and TIME on the Internet ... .

"Speed," our hustle and bustle and stress, doesn't seem to be what the universe aspires to. "Speed" in universe seems to be interpreted as a different kind of "boosting force". And not as a gain / conquest of 3-D-space or market-share in the shortest possible time. What the power of SPACE and TIME looks like has already been shown in the first two books as single formulas representations. The extrapolation and combination of these sizes raise new challenges – and lead to fascinating new solutions.

Before we turn to the so-called "SPEED" as "EFFICIENCY INCREASE", however, we would first like to devote ourselves to further thoughts on SPACE and TIME as such. And to make extrapolations of things, which would have gone beyond the scope of the previous books. Since these extrapolations tend to have the pull of "efficiency increase" or its "prevention", they fit better into this book.

D. SPACE

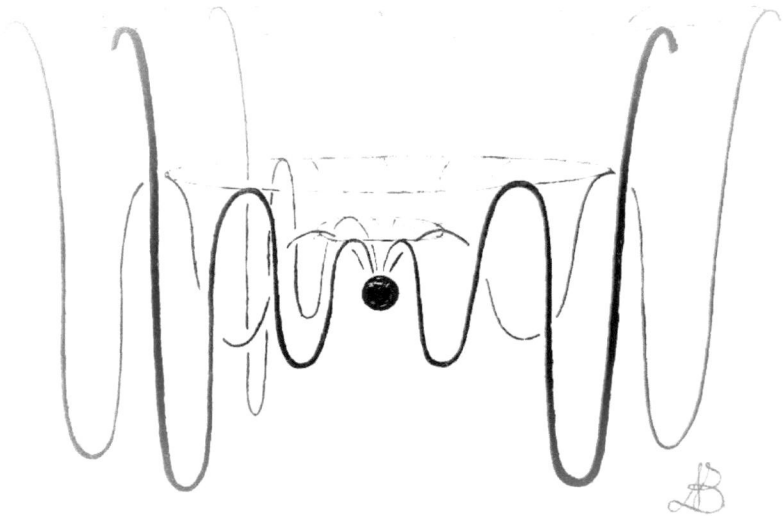

Before we deal with the speed (out of c^2), it is important to penetrate a little bit deeper into its components, so that we can look at everything a little bit more relative later on.

While most people (according to Google images) equate space with a chambre, the space outside that room is many times larger: 50 billion light-years, as diameter of the universe.

We have long suspected that such a powerful dimension must be more than just a "passive" 3-dimensional unit of measurement (height X width X depth). And finally, we were also confirmed by the space formula, which we discovered:

The space formula[02] is (simplified): energy divided by matter:

$$S = \frac{E}{M}$$

This is, first of all, an interesting mathematical result, which has "resulted" from verified formulas (from other physic areas). It additionally is verified by us as plausible in this presented "appearance", because we were able to:
   a. relativize "dark matter" [03]
   b. relativize „dark energy" [03]
   c. disprove Einstein's space curvature via room concentration-aspects[03], and
   d. explain the refraction of light with TIME and SPACE forces[03] instead of space curvature.

Our previous analyses and findings had more to do with the more static aspects of these formulas. Now want to deal with the dynamic aspects of our formulas. Especially since we want to formulate a new formula for "speed" or "effectiveness" as the ultimate goal.

While Albert Einstein was able to explain the "now", we now add the "past" and the "future", dynamically. 😌

D.1. Extrapolation of SPACE

Space can be extrapolated in two ways. With the formula $S = E/M$ you can increase or decrease the E (or what leads to similar effects, increase or decrease the M).

By doing so, we amplify the findings of Albert Einstein. The "Simple Relativity Theory" and the "General Relativity Theory" of Albert Einstein explain the "now" of the universe. We now add the "yesterday" and the "tomorrow". We now can explain mathematically/ astronomically the difference of status of our universe of the "past" and the "present" - and we now additionally can add the "future" to these graphics - see annex.[12]

If the E shrinks because, for example a gas (helium) sun is increasingly turning into a matter-sun, the power of space(-waves) emanating from this sun decreases. The time-force(-waves) (M/E) increase. Doing so, it displaces space. This leads to an increase in light deviation: Light flees to the concentration of space, now further outside, because light progresses faster there. Thus, if light passes a large planet/star, it is not deviated due to a space curvature. But it is a greater concentration of space further away from the star, as already shown in "AstronSpaceOnomy" [03].

As the universe grows, the SPACE must increase. This can only be the case if the E of the counter in the fraction of the SPACE formula increases or/and the M of the denominator becomes smaller.

But if the space grows ever larger, then only energy can exist at the "end of the universe". To increase the power of SPACE, the E must grow constantly bigger - and the M ever smaller. This would mean the "end of the universe" as we know it. But also the "end of time". Time, M/E would be zero divided by infinity – that's zero. The destructive effect of TIME would have been overcome. You could live infinitely. Lamentably you are matter as well. So you won´t exist either, any more. :-(

D.2. SPACE as energy

We can (indirectly) see(!) the ENERGY that emerges from the extrapolated SPACE. It are huge spatial bubbles. And we feel sure, that with our extrapolation of our space-formula, we now decode another spacial-mystery: These "bubbles" are the "voids". And by this, our space-formula is verified by "it is, what you see". 😉

But it's a different kind of space. It's a different kind of energy which "expands" there. It is the space-wave energy of all surrounding galaxies that "concentrates" here. It collects between the galaxies. But also the outermost edge of the universe must consist of this Energy. Between the galaxies we "see" the bubbles as empty spaces, because there is no light reflection at all. But we can´t see this space-energy.

We can´t see these space-waves at the voids. Just as we can´t see the space-concentration, which becomes stronger and stronger, the further away we move from a respective sun/star within a galaxy. The last leads to the phenomenon, we decoded in the last book, AstronSpaceOnomy. Planets, within our constant meter-dimensions, seem to remain constant in their velocity. But measured with SPACE dimensions, they overcome more velocity. Planets de facto fly faster than we see it. In AstronSpaceOnomy, this finding lead to the decoding of the 23% un-known energy, which now explains "dark matter". The planets are not slowed down by "dark matter" gravitation. They don't actually have to fly faster. They fly de facto faster and are not slowed down. Only we can't see it, because we can't see the space waves. This increasing concentration of space-waves, the farer away from the sun, is invisible.

And what we see as bubbles between the galaxies, are also space waves. It is also energy. Another kind of energy or force.

The space bubbles we see are like the expansion of a fire from an explosion – or the vastness of the explosions sound-waves. We measure the strength of a bomb exposure by its destruction, as we can see this. But we hardly measure the area, that the (visible) fire takes from this explosion. Nor do we normally measure the time until we hear the explosion bang. Because humanity´s focus is visibility. The rest is rather "insignificant" for us. And as no one up to us has "looked" closer at possible "space-waves" we were the lucky ones, able to discover the secrets behind the "voids" as well. 😊

D.3. SPACE as a force

It is a space with a lot of power and almost no counter-pole. Almost without time-force, since there is hardly any matter. Hardly or even not at all neutrons, from which (matter) time could act. A space without time has nothing to do with growth, because "growth" can only arise in the course of time. Space here is dimensionless, has nothing to do with 3-D anymore. We only see it large because its energy is so tremendously strong, displacing other things. Here, however, we do not see energy from a bang, but "only" space as "energy". In another form of appearance.

As a force, as the "great" force of space-energy. It is a force because it manages to have this whole "space" for itself. But we only see a bubble in which there is nothing. And we only see this bubble because we see an empty space between the galaxies.

You might also be able to compare the size of this bubble(s) with the display of a weighing machine. The larger the bubble (the force of space), the more the scale would indicate.

If our findings are correct, it should also be the case that the VOIDs are narrower towards the big-bang or large masses of stars/galaxies. And further away from the big-bang or galaxies, towards the outer edge of the universe, the VOIDs should get bigger. Again, astronomers will certainly be able to confirm correlations.

D.3.1. Space in correlation with other findings.

Matter tends to move (Newton). If one hangs a large and a small ball out of e.g. stone next to each other, one can notice that the small ball tilts to the big ball (i.e. hangs crooked). Also the big one will tend to the small, but this inclination is more difficult to see because it is too small. If matter arises, gravity is created. And gravity works everywhere, across all borders. Matter will always tend to move, because there are always some gravitational waves somewhere.

Without space, however, this movement of both spheres to each other would not be possible. Space makes this movement possible. Space must therefore be more dominant than matter (and gravity ... and time ...). This is also the case, because the space formula is "S = E/M" – and ...

1.) at the big-bang (as it still is today) there was more (free) energy, than (in) matter (bounded energy) – i.e.:

2.) space must also be greater than time (T = M/E) – according to which it might be possible, that the universe exists since 13.8 billion years. But, on the other hand, universe has a diameter of 50 billion light-years (which we will put into perspective later) ..., and ...

3.) Gravity is in "visual" space only an underpower of matter. In the black hole, however, gravity is stronger than matter – and also stronger than space (see later).

4.) Gravity, also results (in "visual" space) from the formula of the SPACE: Matter is in the denominator – and as

   a. Matter is continuously diminishing and

b. gravity is only a part of matter …

… at the outer edge of universe, SPACE is stronger than gravity.

All is relative, and changing in the corresponding areas 😉

This example appears in the end result as "static". The balls remain in their slightly oblique position. But the force of gravity continues to work – thanks to the liberty providing force of space. Energy "flows" (S=E/M). Without this constant "flowing" energy, space would not exist. The space, gives the two spheres the possibility to move to each other and to remain separated from each other "in space". On the other hand, in a certain way, space is depending as well from that gravity waves. It´s depending on (at the outer edges of universe) a minimal quantity of matter – and gravity – for not imploding. It's a give and take.

Without the ever-present and flowing energy of space, we and all the rest of the universe would not exist.

However, space not only enables standstill – and also, thanks to the gravity of two stones, their possibility to move to each other. But, what space seems to promote primarily is movement. Space promotes exactly the opposite of the standstill of the two balls facing each other. Space in our universe promotes the drifting apart of everything, rather than the standstill and moving towards each other of the two balls.

D.4. SPACE as vacuum

What is an empty space? A "bubble" without any amount of air or matter? Yes, a vacuum. And what force results from a vacuum? Have you ever closed the valve of an bycilcle-air pump and then created a vacuum by pulling away the pump lever? The result is an enormous under-pressure, which sucks back the lever that created the vacuum. Yes, a vacuum creates a suction effect.

And in universe, it's nothing else. A space without any amount of matter nor neutrons is the most glaring vacuum that exists.

In the outermost part of the universe, where there is hardly (no) matter left, there exists an extreme vacuum. An extreme force of the SPACE-dimension.

And also in the "voids" between the galaxias, where there is nothing visible in those bubbles, there is a vacuum. In those places the space-energy waves of the galaxias collide together and displace everything of matter and TIME. There exists an extreme force of the dimension SPACE. Matter is displaced because space wants to be pure SPACE. Aspires to be "pure" energy.

Voids and the outer edge of the universe are nothing but huge areas of energy in the form of space-vacuum. We see large "bubbles" between the galaxies because we are used to seeing in "space" dimensions. However, these bubbles are empty, a vacuum. And therefore not to be understood as a "material 3-D dimension". They are nothing more than a force, an energy. We cannot see the vacuum-energy-force of the universe-edge by nature, because it has no limitation by one or more other galaxies, as with the voids. But if we extrapolate SPACE, then at the end of universe, there must be that vacuum. Like in the voids.

The fact that we see nothing in these areas of space is due to the power of the energy prevailing there. Each matter is shredded – it is converted into energy according to the formula ($S = E/M$) in order to further increase the power of the SPACE-dimension. Matter is sucked in, to generate more space out of it, in order to further grow space-energy.

So, matter is not only converted by the "black holes" via their "gravitational power" in order to grow. Also "black bubbles", voids, and their "absorption power" convert matter, for own growth.

But: while the shredding of matter in "black holes" can now be observed very well, the "conversion" of matter into SPACE-energy still owes the astronomical verification. This, up to now, can only be shown as an extrapolation from the formula. Furthermore, what we see is a space without any matter at all – while in "normal" universe at least there exists on average one neutron per cubic meter. For both aspects our defined formula also makes sense.

The galaxies that are sucked in by these forces are currently not (yet) torn apart (as a galaxy) and shredded, because they hold together (yet) by their gravitational forces. However, the individual galaxies as such are very much separated by these void-forces between them - and can thus go their own ways without collisions. 😉 .

Thus, it are not only the planets (as to Einstein) which optimized their own routes. But it are as well complete galaxies, which look for their own ways, by "feeding" the voids with SPACE-waves from their "body-masses". 😉

The growth-power of the universe seems to be potentiated by our defined efficiency multiplier (z^2 - see later) - and primarily by its SPACE component. SPACE seems to be stronger than the force of gravity of the material part of the universe – and even as its "black-holes".

The universe is (apparently) getting bigger and bigger. But that's just because we can see better than we can measure… The vacuums (seems to) pull the visible galaxies apart on all sides. Out, into the open space.

What we can't see, or at least haven't counted yet is: How much of the planets and stars disappear into "black bubbles" (voids) at the same time. Just because even the realization of the aspect, that (almost) every galaxy has an own black hole, is very fresh. And our findings have just been published.

We are not yet in a position to measure what has disappeared in black holes as a total. And even less are able to measure disappeared galaxies in "black bubbles".

Therefore, the question arises, whether the universe (as an addition of growth and shrinkage) "overall" really "expands". What is the sum of:
- The drifting apart of the galaxies;
- The possible destruction in voids;
- The shrinkage due to black-holes
- The destruction in black-holes; and
- The birth of new stars out of nebulae) ???
Perhaps the universe even shrinks "overall" due to matter disappearing on both sides ...

Furthermore, we are only able to see a finite distance with our telescopes. From a certain distance, a "wall" is created. Until recently, this wall only allowed us to discover 100 billion galaxies. In the meantime, we can look so far, that we can see 400 billion galaxies.

But the "view" is not only limited to the optical limits. According to our extrapolations, the space vacuum, from a certain limit onwards. sucks the planets outward into the "unknown" space. This happens faster than the speed of light (of our actual measuring, without considering SPACE-concentration aspects). Thus, also faster, than the light of stars, which is (also) send to "back" - towards our viewing direction. Thus, we will not be able to see all these extreme fast flying stars and galaxies at all - as we need light, to be able to watch extremes. Other energy waves are too slow.

With this "fast" it may also be possible to keep the stars "only" being pushed out into space at the speed of light (according to our calculation). But in this area of the universe, the space waves (distances) are relatively shorter than in our "latitudes". And with that, the stars fly faster than at the speed of the light, which we know.

They take (keep) their light with them. And in empty space (in an absolute vacuum, consisting only out of energy) light (photons) will have no "space" to expand, but will be teared to nothingness because of the vacuum. This is the opposite aspect, of light being absorbed by an extreme black-holes, where the gravity and TIME push away SPACE, and no light is able to find its way out of the black-hole.

In this respect, our guess is that from a certain optical distance AND from a certain SPACE-energy-force-constellation we are no longer be able to "see" what is happening behind this universe boundaries. We cannot "see" what is happening behind the black hole. Nor can we see, what happens behind the speed-wall nor behind the "black-holes", the voids.

What happens behind the universe boundaries might be seen, if researchers examine our new aspects in the voids (the "black bubbles"), parallel to the examinations of what happens with the matter destroyed at "black holes".

D.5. SPACE as optical illusion

The fact that SPACE allows or/and promotes drifting apart can be seen at the fact that the universe is expanding (apparently) constantly - and faster. Faster than it could be made plausible with previous calculating methods.

Speed is according to our earthly ideas "space per time", km/h. However, this earthly thinking results primarily from the material orientation of mankind: space as meters of a chamber – and time as an indication on a clock.

However, the universe sees our "speed" more as a "multiplier" with two power poles (SPACE and TIME):

1. SPACE (room) is energy divided by matter ($S = E/M$), which leads to increasing energy when matter decreases (i.e. space acts mainly as a force – and not only as a 3-D size) and thus leads to a primary energetic "strengthening" and not necessarily to spatial "expansion".

2. TIME is matter divided by energy ($T = M/E$), which leads to a "weakening" of the dimension TIME when matter decreases or/and energy rises.

3. Thus, it may as well come to a double multiplicative effect (more SPACE power in less TIME power) of the multiplier (our "dynamic c^2"). Not as "speed", but rather as energy.

4. More ("visible" free) SPACE (in the voids) strengthens (energetically) our visible universe (and weakens the destructive forces of the TIME) By doing so, it appears to us, that the universe is growing far faster, than in reality.

5. Relativization of the "visible" spatial extension

   a. We see the VOIDs as a great space, because we can see the "energetic-forces-effects(!)" of SPACE "randomly" as shadows between the galaxies.

b. But a shadow is not a space – and extremely relative: if the sun is above us, our shadow is very small. If the sun stays horizontal to us, our shadow is infinite.

c. A shadow as well, like energy, is nothing "tangible". Thus, we should not regard the "size" of the "VOIDs shadow" as a 3-D-size, according to our (materially oriented) mathematical rules.

Because the "size" we see as a bubble between the galaxies is mathematically a shadow: nothing! Because there is no matter in this bubble – it is an absolute vacuum. And SPACE is energy divided by matter: $S = E / M$. But if there is no matter, then there is a zero under the breaking line. And according to our (earthly material) mathematics rules, a number divided by zero is: nothing. Thus, this bubble, this VOID, must not be "considered" under 3-D-space-dimensional aspects. But "only" as an energetic force.

d. This is now, as well mathematically, clarifying that great mystery of VOIDs ☺ .

e. We can see these large bubbles with an extreme vacuum, the VOIDs, because it is an energetic force between the galaxies, which "presents" itself to us as a big bubble. De facto, however, it is an optical illusion, an energetic effect.

f. The reverse optical illusion of this phenomenon is the phenomenon of the "black hole". While the VOID acts expansive and appears visually large, the "black hole" acts contractionary and appears - compared to the energetic forces that act there - as quite small.

g. We "see" two opposing "spatial" expressions or phenomena of forces (energies), because previous astronomers have defined space as "static" - and (yet) not relative. And as well because the space is only visible for us in a 3-dimensional way. We cannot see the energetic dimension (the "waves") of the SPACE – but only the effects:

a. galaxies pulled to all sides and outwards. And since the energy "waves" of the SPACE are extremely concentrated in the VOID, we see the VOID as large.

b. And since the space waves at the BLACK-HOLE are very wide (the energetic force of SPACE is extremely small, because here, the energetic force of gravity and TIME displace SPACE), we see the "black hole" as relatively small – in relation to the tremendous forces that work there.

h. The "optical effect" of the SPACE dimension (in close correlation with the forces of TIME) is thus comparable to a telescope: from one end we see everything bigger and closer when looking through. But if we look through from the other side of the telescope, everything seems smaller and farther away. Both look throughs lead to an optical illusion: that something is closer or more distant than it is "factual"*. ☺ (*According to quantum theory, however, everything could be considered "factually correct" – and here, there, or farther…).

i. Last not least: the "energetic effect" of the "SPACE"-dimension is comparable to the "optical telescope-effect" of the 3-D "space" dimension.

D.6. Unmasking "dark energy"

A space without any "matter" is nothing more than a vacuum. And a vacuum is a force that can do work: sucking. That is energy(!), power. Voids are extrapolated SPACE – matter converted into energy. If space is a goal of the universe - as it grows faster than we can calculate -, then, in our equation S =

E/M, the energy must constantly rise or/and matter must constantly decrease. At some point, E is so large or/and M so small that it leads to: S = E. SPACE is an energy, a force - a force to do "work". SPACEs work is to achieve "growth". "Growth" is one of the main goals of the universe, at least for the time being – and at least in the area we primarily (can) consider.

Hereby we solve the phenomenon, which accounts for 72% of the total energy of the universe: the "dark energy". SPACE is the answer to the question why the universe grows faster than all current mathematical approaches "allow". It is due to the power of a vacuum, which results from the formula of the SPACE, which can be extrapolated to the total energy of the universe. 😉

The extrapolated SPACE is as powerful as all the energy of the universe. In the end, universe seems to become an absolute vacuum. Seems, but it's not. In our opinion, this process stops at a certain limit. But this would go beyond our actual scope (the search for efficiencies).

The property of a vacuum is to suck. And so the voids between the galaxias suck these galaxias apart – and thus prevent many collisions in an extremely efficient way. Each galaxy can go its own way. These voids are so large, that, although they "suck" the galaxies, there are hardly any collisions of galaxies. Their size tends to cause the galaxies to move away from each other. Especially because there are different voids between the galaxies.

Since SPACE and TIME have opposing formulas, they compete against each other. One can also define that SPACE "displaces" TIME in the voids and at the outer edge of the universe. In other words, one can define that SPACE wants to "go its own way", "want to have its freedom". And "flees" from the areas of the galaxies "infected" with TIME (where there is matter, gravity and TIME are there as well). SPACE does not want (and can´t) "unfold" there (in the universe areas of galaxies filled with TIME, matter, and gravity) – and "tends" away from galaxies.

However, "fleeing" can also be a "pushing away". The closer to a strong gravitational field (e.g. a large galaxy or black hole) the weaker or farther away a potential VOID would be. This still needs to be explored. But the tendency is there. Voids become larger the farer away they are from the galaxies (and their corresponding galaxy-black-holes).

Voids are something like intermediate stations or/and have direct channels to the outer areas of the universe, towards this energy seems to flow. And this "current" flow outwards, "rips" - as a vacuum - the galaxies with them, outwards.

This is an extremely efficient growth, without as many collisions as they occur on Earth in the realization of the current models of economy and society. (Note: it's not about earthly(!) 3-D-space-gain, but about energetic(!) SPACE-gain).

D.7. The universe "reduction"

In our opinion, however, the universe does not (!) "grow" as strongly as the current calculations of astronomy (with standard values / constants) represent. And it is smaller than the 50 billion lightyears valid today. The voids are empty (vacuum) – similar to the "space" at the far end of the universe. And the calculated dimensions of the voids are "measurably" energy. Based on the size of the voids, we should be able to determine how much energy is in them. What we (still) regard as a big bubble is nothing but (converted) energy – and thus nothing any more mysterious. But it's not a 3-D space. SPACE-energy is extremely concentrated here. And when a star approaches such areas, its light appears as purple as if it moves extremely quick away and almost getting faster. But the star moves with far less speed than calculated and does not increase velocity in the way we calculate at the moment. It are just the closer space-waves, which lead to purple light – and when the waves get more concentrated, the light gets even more purple-color.

The star, de facto, only "crosses" space energy waves (in the voids or at the edge of space), which lie much closer together. This can not be considered, when calculating with constant(!) "meters" or "light-years". We think the star moves away extremely fast, but it moves as fast as ever – only the speed (constant km per h), which we have set (color purple XX represents velocity YY), are no longer correct at highly concentrated space-energy waves. The color gets brighter because the space-waves distances get shorter. But as to our speed definition, the star keeps flying at the same velocity. We only think the star is moving faster and faster and the universe is growing faster and faster, but the facto only the concentration of space increases at the outer edge of space – and everything grows "normally".

It remains to be seen, whether these SPACE-formula aspects of voids and universe edge are enough to represent the 72% of unknown forces, that cause the universe to seemingly grow so "rapidly".

The dimension of the universe, these 50 billion light-years, could thus shrink into the same dimension that we defined as the age of the universe. The universe is 13.8 billion years old – and 13.8 billion light-years "large" (when the constant "meters" is relativized by the current environmental forces of the SPACE). At least things tend towards this findings. Because Einstein has added a square to the c. What this means will be clarified later in this book when it comes up to "speed": that (mankind) "construction" representing "(mankind) space divided by (mankind) time".

The areas of 3-D-"spaces" of all galaxies are a miniature compared to the areas filled with space-energy waves at voids or the area at the universe-edge. And galaxies themselves do not grow as fast as the universe over all.

The universe has astronomically recognized that free space promotes crisis-free "growth". It preserves its matter from colliding in order to be able to continue growing. Collisions are more probable within the galaxies, where there is not as much SPACE-power as outside.

We may compare the outer surroundings with "economics" – and the space within galaxies with "business". And while universe is expanding for more liberty and peace of all galaxies, mankind is tending towards the black-holes in their corresponding galaxies: destroying its own environment – and concentrating power at only one point.

Unfortunately, the "homo-sapiens" is not yet ready to recognize the "suck-effects" of new ideas (energies) from free "spaces" for all mankind as the best demand-pull that exists. Nor does humanity underpin all positive aspects with feasibilities to realization. We added solutions to these dilemmas in our books AstronTimeOnomy and AstronSpace-Onomy[02].

SPACE is an elementary component for efficiency. Also and especially for the "clocked" industrial world. Because here, unfortunately, the time-clock (i.a. via materialistic rationalizations) and the gravitational-clock (concentration) are destroying many things.

Universe is smaller, than we think. And universe knows, that it is not all about 3-D-size. There are far better ways to achieve "size" (wealth), than being the biggest, or getting the most. Universe concentrates on efficient energetic-space-dimensions. Energy replaces – and does not need much - 3-D-space. Our comparison on earth is the intelligence (energy) within a (3-D) brain. The brain does not need to grow. But the intelligence inside can grow. More "intel-ligence" for all mankind leads to far better results, than more "market share" for just some companies or persons (at the expense of our environment).

D.8. SPACE in-definiteness of universe?

The extrapolation of SPACE, $S = E / M$, according to actual trends, ends in the equation $S = E$, when (nearly) all matter has converted into energy.

In this constellation TIME ($T = M / E$) has no effect. Zero divided by infinity keeps zero. There exists only the energy of the "space". The energy out of the "SPACE"-forming energy". And thus, without time, the state of infinity will be valid. Life, however, without matter, will no longer exist there.

D.9. SPACE, the end of the universe?

If the extrapolation of the space equation $S = E/M$ ends in the equation $S = E$. Then, there would be an absolute vacuum. This vacuum could not be further developed, because there is no longer any matter whose energy could be used for further growth. And a vacuum without any thrust nor pull forces which could sustain it as a vacuum, should actually implode. However, since this vacuum is full of energy waves that seemingly act more independently than anything else, that exists in space, at the end, it may also be possible, that space continues to exist as a large balloon full of energy, cross-waving from one side to the other.

D.10. Space as inner- & outer connected spiral – our books front-picture.

At the moment we see space growing. Like the growing circles, starting in one of the directions of the inner spiral of our books front-drawing. We don't believe, that all matter will end in energy, as space is always looking to balance forces. Therefore, at the outside edge of our universe there might be a frontier of nothingness, when all matter would be turned to energy. But before reaching that frontier, the space waves might as well "overflow" and circle back/down at the outside of all the happenings of our watchable universe. Back and down, outside. And at a certain point, the tremendous gravitational forces of the "other" sides of the black-holes may be "attracting" those space-waves. Back to the above mentioned start. Bringing back the energy, which got lost at the initial front-side of the black holes. And with this energy, possibly circumventing the blackholes, new stars may arise by a kind of cosmic wind, resulting from the coming back SPACE-waves, which press together cosmic dust. And the double-spiral restarts time and again. This matches the requirements of actual astronomy-status-quo, that Energy is limited – and always present, in the one or the other forms. A perfect perpetuum mobile. ☺

D.11. The Universe-Space-Energy-Pull as a mission statement for earthly demand suck

In the book "AstronSpaceOnomy" we have used the effects of space in astronomy as a model for better sociology, for more freedom and peace in the world, because the coexistence of galaxies, stars and planets in the universe works better than the coexistence and paths of humans on Earth.

With the now extrapolated aspects of the SPACE dimension, two further meanings are added to the SPACE: 1.) a multiplicative and 2.) an efficiency-enhancing function.

1.) Multiplicative aspects

    1.a. In the universe:

Our SPACE-formula increases the growth of the universe by many times more of that, what astronomers have been able to mathematically calculate on the basis of current know-how. This results thanks to discovery of the "vacuum" filled with "energy" and its "suction power".

1.b. Transferred to earthly aspects:

In our brains we also have a lot of (energetic) "space". Since we use very little capacity of our brain, it could also be defined as a quasi "vacuum". And our brain, like the vacuum of the universe, is not an absolute vacuum, but full of energy.

The more this brain is filled with knowledge, the more it can find things that interest it. And through his desires, a huge demand surge can arise, which would have an enormous, multiplicative expansion effect on the growth of our economy.

Everyone could also realize his demand requirements if the LAZEB (life-working-time-unit-bonus-concept of the book "AstronTime-Onomy"[01] would be implemented. At last, the long-awaited demand would be present in order to be able to solve all the current problems.

DIGRESSION

Yes, with our astronomy-based models, we want to optimize the prosperity of nations. However, this should not be at the expense of our environment. If all mankind would live like the Americans, we would need 5 earths - and for the European standard of living, we would need 3 earths.

In astronomy, everything is energy, including matter. The only energy similar to the extremely efficient energy from the "SPACE"; - being like a vacuum charged with energy - is the energy in our brains. Knowledge and intelligence, however, is not enough – in a world as it is today - to achieve a similar status to that of the SPACE in the universe. On Earth, we also need financial (play-)space – and as well more freedom. Both can be achieved with the LAZEB model.

With wisdom and LAZEB, every person can reach Maslow´s pyramide-of-needs-PEAK(!): transcendence. This is done primarily via 1.) Education (mental ENERGY) and by 2.) simultaneous (primarily economic) independence (own path to be achievable).

The higher people are based on the Maslow pyramid, the more sustainable they will be.

Knowledge is a fascinating commodity – and the only resource that increases with consumption without destroying the environment. Knowledge-space or know-ledge-energy-expansion instead of commodity-consumption-"intoxication" is an aspect that needs to be pushed much more in order to optimize our world.

DIGRESSION-END

2.) Efficiency-enhancing aspects
2.a. In the Universe

The part of the universe we primarily consider is "expanding" strongly. "SPACE"(-energy) is an elementary goal of space. Matter, on the other hand, currently has only a significance of 4.6% of total energy in space – with a decreasing tendency (when extrapolating SPACE).[12]

Due to the suction of the galaxies by different voids, as well as those of the outer vacuum at the edge of space, there are relatively few collisions in space – in contrast to earthly human economic and sociology models …

2.b. On Earth

Due to limited CAPITAL resources, the realization of own paths by states (stars) or by companies or private people (planets) are extremely limited on Earth – in contrast to the possibilities in universe with its SPACE-energy and the "start-energy" for stars.

But also KNOW-HOW instances on earth limit possibilities: Primary universities/ professors define the current "standard" – and mainly this standard counts for the "normal" financing of growth projects. However, knowledge doubles every two years – but the number of professors or universities does not. We have a status, similar to that when the Church still defined the "knowledge standard" – and slowed down development.

"Familiar" "mater" or "technic" (goods) count more than new "intangible" aspects (knowhow). This is exactly the opposite of the expansion successes of the universe!

The fact that knowledge energy (the power to do work) cannot be patented (at least not directly, and at least not in Europe) shows humanity's focus on the material aspects, which innovations are patentable. If only material ideas can secure survival, the chances of good ideas are poor. Being published at all is the first challenge. But without a patent they may be copied from everyone, without securing survival needs of the inventor. Most people can't afford to spend a lot of time on an idea. Or/and: They keep the idea by themselves, before others steal this idea. And these others, thanks to may be more time or/and money, expand and implement it accordingly – without paying any reward. Thus, many people keep their ideas hidden. Maybe they can do something with it later. Later. Often never. Missed chances!

On earth, crises occur again and again. Why not adopt the success models of the universe?

Now, however, we also want to deal in more detail with the second aspect of "speed", TIME.

E. TIME

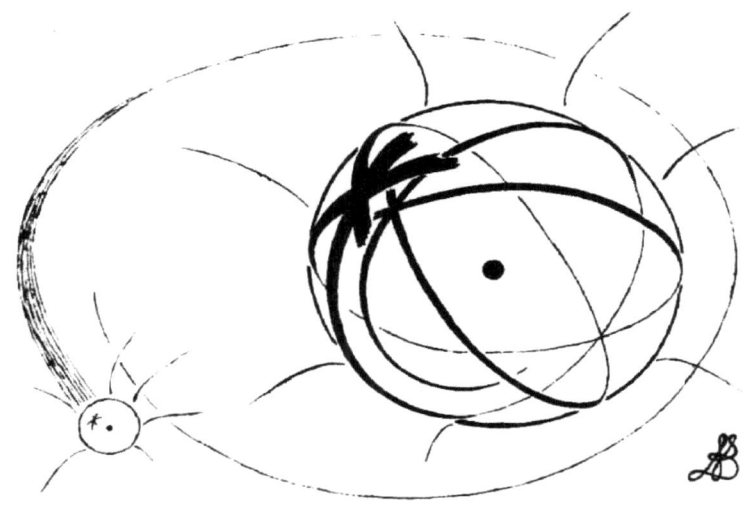

Time (see AstronTimeOnomy[01]) is (simplified) matter divided by energy:

$$T = \frac{M}{E}$$

In the following we would like to present, with further thoughts on TIME, why our TIME (and

SPACE) formulas make sense. And as well, we will interpret previous experiments in a different way.

E.1. Extrapolation of TIME

a) Time at the edge of the (material) universe

As space grows, the development of the power of TIME must decrease.

The universe can only "grow" when SPACE increases – and this can only be when the energy rises or/and matter shrinks at the SPACE-formula: $S = E / M$. The TIME force therefore must shrink continuously because of its formula: $T = M / E$.

Time is less strong, less active, less concentrated or only minimally present at the edge of the (material) universe.

At the outside edge of the universe, where hardly any matter seems to exist anymore, life seems to become infinite, as time no longer has power. But going with the extrapolation of time, takes so much time, that we surely will not be living any more. And:

if at the universe edge there should not be any matter any more, we as well will be dead. So, why wait so long? The same aspects above mentioned must also apply to the voids, between the galaxies. And they are present today. That is, we wouldn't have to fly so far and so long to the end of the universe to only theoretically become immortal. If we manage to penetrate into the voids between our galaxies, we could live endlessly. It would certainly require space capsules that can withstand the extreme tearing forces of an extreme vacuum. But without any other time, or material or gravitational force, which are destructive, we could live endlessly.

Steven Hawking has suspected a similar effect[08], which arises when travelling in space at the speed of light. However, its derivation resulted from a paradox, which could not be clarified at that time, but which we were able to clarify in AstronSpaceOnomy[02] – and just briefly presented here again. At voids, endless life can be possible, without needing to achieve light speed. That, what was nearly impossible to be achieved with standard meters dimensions, can now be achieved, due to concentrated space-waves, energy, quite "near", at voids: endless life ☺

b) TIME within the universe ...

Within the universe in which we also live on our Earth, TIME is one of the components, one of the forces.

In the formula, $T = M/E$, it is revealed that TIME is matter-immanent. That means, that TIME is only ever as strong as the respective matter for which it acts.
But TIME has nothing to do with "having time". TIME is destructive. In the universe, and on earth:

- A star with very much TIME-power means, that the matter of this time carrier must be extremely large. And with further growth, extreme gravity and a super-nova implosion will result. A destruction of the material towards dust or a quasar, or also a black hole is possible. All energy might be squeezed out of the matter. For all a.m. alternatives, however, TIME is also weekend or destroyed. When the M is destroyed, TIME becomes zero.

- Too much time-"pressure" at humans, has to do with dealing with too much (material ...) tasks. Being over-loaded, sooner or later there will come a burnout. People then will vegetate around like a quasar. Or will even die. No time for that person will be there anymore. And body-matter rots, energy gets out of the body (matter...).

"Having time" is a misinterpretation of the dimensions. Our imagination-pictures concerning "SPACE" (chamber) and "TIME" (clocks) show again, how little we really deal with these extremely important dimensions. By "I have time" we actually mean "to have (free) space". This is the opposite of "having time". Much time in its physical dimension leads to stress. And, too much matter and too little energy, leads to act efficiently.

c) Time as matter ... or gravity ...

If at $T = M/E$ the entire E disappears and only M remains, the result is the equation: $M/0$! And a number divided by zero is nothing. That is: everything collapses, when there is no or only too little energy. It comes to the super nova. M without E cannot live because time does not allow her. But: energy can´t "die" – must keep existing! That's an essential law! The energy of matter is released during the super-nova in/explosion – and either ...

1. "returned" back as energy to the rest of the universe - for other purposes (e.g. growth ...), or
2. Used to build a quasar, or – especially with large (ex-)stars ...
3. converted into gravitational force of a new "black hole".

The fact that extrapolated gravity from any matter has the same force (energy) as the energy that comes from Einstein by multiplying matter by c^2 is demonstrated in my book "Astronomic Solutions" [09]

d) TIME over time

According to the above chapter "c)", TIME seems to be "cleanse" or destructive in the case of too little energy (e.g. due to age) in matter and humans. This can be quite efficient. Matter that can no longer fulfil its mission to indirectly generate more space waves, because it lacks of the energy to do so, can be "disposed" of in a "black hole" (grave).

People, YOU, should free them-(your-)selve(s) from too many tasks (material). And devote them-(your-)selve(s) as long as possible, to energetic aspects (knowledge, advice, experience, etc.). And specially: delegate!!! – give SPACE to others, like stars push the voids!!!, by spreading SPACE energy towards them. Do not take too much care of all things, by only yourself, when the "time pressure" (because of your(!) "gravity", - too much "matter/tasks" being "transferred to you) begins to gnaw at you") becomes too strong. Otherwise, you will experience a "burn-out" or death faster than you would like.

According to the above chapter "b)" time in normal life is a constant companion. Especially in industrialized worlds, where everything is clocked. Because capital market rules dictate this, stress is a fact everywhere. Stress – certainly is good for his capital concerns. But if all people only walk in the hamster wheel, then no new paths arise. Obtaining free space, especially for new knowledge, is one of the most important aspects of our current lives. Universe predicts!

Where time is "restrained", aspects of the above chapter "a)" are valid. Space waves. That is, energy is what the universe aspires. And here the destructive time has nothing to look for. As a result, more and more "free""space" is created in the universe, which allows the planets, stars and galaxies to go their own ways, without colliding.

From this point "a)" humanity can learn a lot of efficiency in terms of human knowledge. Knowledge is for humanity, similar to SPACE-energy for the universe. Lamentably people also act in the field of knowledge under the pressure of time - which the universe "knowingly" does not do. Free-space waves "growth"-energy is too important for SPACE as to allow TIME-energy to be present here. If humanity would educate itself more and everywhere, and if there were more "space" for further education as well in professional life, the prosperity of nations would be many times greater than it is at present. And all would be much more efficient than with the current extremely timed time-orientations. If you have to terminate your study in 3 years, many students only learn by heart. Knowing the depths of aspects would be far more efficient. Even if it takes some semesters on top. Intelligence leads to more efficiency, than "just" know-how.

F. The correlations between space and time

F.1. General aspects

It is important to note that both TIME and in particular SPACE (e.g. collision-free) ensure extreme efficiency in our universe. The fact that for the universe the relatively passive matter is not so important (it accounts for only 4.6% of the space-energy) is now understandable, as the force-dimensions of SPACE and TIME have become more plastic. And that the material (and time-centered) focusing of mankind makes little sense, now, also becomes clear – at least if efficiency and sustainability are of interest.

Through our SPACE and TIME approaches, we are in the process of uncovering 95% of the previously unexplored energies.

SPACE and TIME are extreme efficiency drivers. We should involve them – and their correlations – much more in our reflections. More than the "simple" focus on matter around which, up to now, almost all astronomy – and unfortunately also economy – has so far moved. The universe is "miles ahead" of us with its SPACE and TIME aspects ...

In particular, there seems to be a starkly difference between the goals of the universe and those of humanity. As universe tends towards "space", humanity tends toward "time". Everything has to be faster and earlier and achieve ever more and better results. For real and better efficiency and sustainability, this approach seems to be the wrong orientation. This time-orientation may be "due" to "natural correlations". Time is (technically, as formula) closer to the material orientation of mankind. But, in efficiency aspects, the spatial orientation is miles ahead of the time-orientation. This can be learned from the existence and expansion of the universe ...

Einstein's c^2 is many times more important (square-potency) for the energy generation of the simple relativity, than all the material things mankind aspires. Unfortunately, humans have also focused on the wrong component in our "dynamized c^2": time rather than space. And lamentably, there is not only the wrong focusing, but as well there are wrong pictures about importance.
Concerning "space" mankind only thinks at chambers, or wars for territories - thus focuses only on 3-D-aspects, instead of looking at energetic aspects. And concerning "time" the pictures just see material 3-D-clocks, instead of seeing the destructive aspects of time, specially, when cooperating with too much matter – and its gravity.

F.2. Formula engineering

Space and time work, judging by their formulas, in opposite directions.

Many facts suggest that this correlation is correct:

- The destructive effect of time: time becomes the greater (more powerful, more destructive) the less "power" (energy) is present. The time formula "T = M/E" predicts this).
  - The greater the power of matter, the greater the destructive influence of gravity and time
  - The smaller the power of energy, the greater the influence of time
  - The more matter, the more gravity
  - The more gravity the more likely it is to create a super-nova-destruction and a "black hole"
  - Super-Nova and black-hole also destroy the power of time, because time is "carrier-immanent": without matter, no time.
  - When time is destroyed, space (in the immediate vicinity) is also destroyed, as both are connected and correlated multiplicatively: $0 \times \infty = 0$!
  - When space is destroyed, the base for orbits (etc. see later) is

also destroyed – and more and more planets and stars plunge into the black hole.
- o The fact that there is only a limited catastrophe – around the black hole – is due to the fact that all other stars and galaxies refill this "spaceless room" with their SPACE-energy-waves.

- However, the destructive effect of time is currently seemingly overcompensated by the "constructive" effect of space. The universe is growing.
  - o As space grows, the result of the space formula "R = E/M" - must grow.
    - ✦ More energy is being generated at the moment, and/or
    - ✦ Matter must be deminished at the moment
    - ✦ "Space" gets bigger
  - o If we look at the comparison from Wikipedia[12], the "dark energy" has grown to 72% of the total energy from 380,000 years after the Big

Bang to the present day (13.8 billion years later).

- ✦ As the universe grows - and
- ✦ since energy is the main growth aspect of space ...
- ✦ the "dark energy" seems to be primarily traceable to our formula of space.

- "Space" grows ...
  - o The ultraviolet light from 'removing' stars says the space of the universe is expanding according to the current interpretation of 'speed'
  - o Even if "space" is viewed at, primarily from the "energetic" (SPACE waves) aspect, instead of the "material" (3-D) perspective, it is the case that this dimension increases.
  - o At the same time, however, this means that the dimension of time - and its powers - is diminishing.

✦ so, if the destructive forces of time (M/E) decrease because the energy is rising, then – at least in the outer part of the universe – infinite life could be possible. Lamentably here no matter is present any more – so we would be dead as well …

✦ But: the same constellation applies for voids. They are closer. We just need rockets, that withstand the vacuum at that places …

F.3. Relativity of SPACE and TIME

F.3.1. The Relativity of SPACE

F.3.1.0. The meter - the measure of all things?

The base of the dimension space is defined in astronomy as "meter", m. This is a constant – and constants are "inviolable", as we already had to learn when we developed our

TIME and SPACE formulas out of Einstein´s "c²" (at that time, still a constant).

Yes, in order to be able to calculate at all, it is important to assume a basis. But...

F.3.1.0.a. The base
The base "m" is an earthly measure – the 10 millionth part of the distance from the pole to the equator on our "Earth" (calculated today somewhat more complex, but here it is irrelevant).

F.3.1.0.b. The relative importance
The Earth is just a planet from only our solar system (just one of 100 billion stars, just and only in our galaxy "Milk Way"). In the universe there are another (currently estimated) 400 billion galaxies of 100 billion stars + X trillion planets.

For the rest of the universe, "m" is not a value that is valid as a "standard".

F.3.1.0.c. The measurement

Meter "m" suggests to us (with unscrupulous recognition as standard, which also applies throughout the universe) that the universe has a diameter (space) of 50 billion lightyears - although it is only 13.8 billion years old (time).

F.3.1.0.d. Relativization of the space-unit "meter" "m"

If energy and matter are relative according to Einstein, then the SPACE must also be relative, according to our SPACE formula $R = E / M$. One meter is not everywhere the same dimension (and a second is not everywhere a second, see below). The "constant" unit of measure "meter" is sometimes larger and sometimes smaller. Their size depends to a large extent on the surroundings. The more the "energy" determines the environment, the greater and more powerful the SPACE power becomes (and the longer/ weaker a time wave will get – thus, lifetime will increase).

In the process, the astronomical "constant" "meter" completely loses its significance as a "measurement unit". Space in the universe has quite little to do with the 3-D constant "meter" that we use on Earth. At maximum in the matter, "M" of the "denominator", there is still a kind of "meter", but in the counter the energy dominates. More important than the measurement the unit "meter" is the correlation of the environment from energy and matter.

Already in the last book, AstronSpaceOnomy, we demonstrated, that SPACE, the further away from the star, becomes more concentrated – and could thereby relativize the "dark matter", "rectify" the space and explain the refraction of light by SPACE & TIME forces, rather than via space bending.

F.3.2. The reality of SPACE (the formula within time-comparison with visible aspects)

The SPACE-force ($S = E / M$) - which is primarily coupled with ENERGY – today, is (purely "visually", i.e. 3-dimensional consideration) a multiple "greater" than the TIME-force ($T = M / E$) which is primarily linked to MATTER.

The SPACE-force also seems to grow faster than the TIME-force. And since both are correlated with each other ($S * Z = 1$) the TIME has to get smaller.

The extrapolation of SPACE resulted (see above) in $R = E$. And if all matter were (close) to disappear, the value for TIME ($T = M/E$) would be (close to) 0 (zero). The fact that we tend to be right here, can now be derived from another phenomenon:

Graphics and info from "Wikipedia"

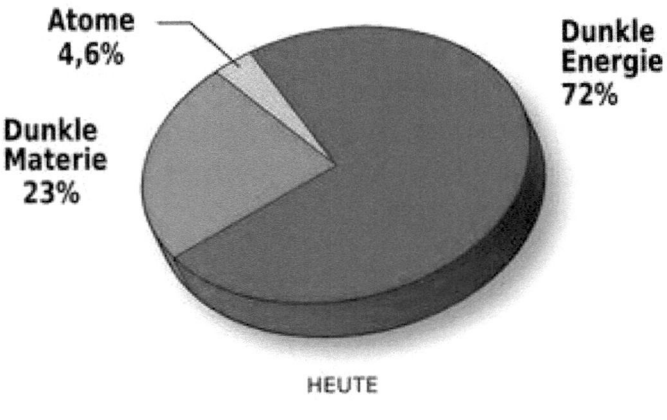

Atome
4,6%

Dunkle
Materie
23%

Dunkle
Energie
72%

HEUTE

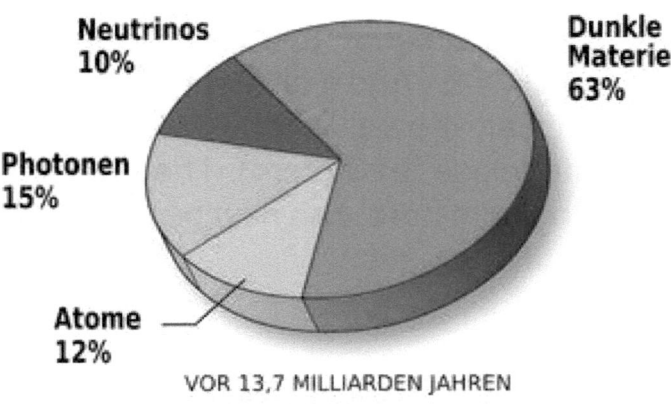

Neutrinos
10%

Photonen
15%

Atome
12%

Dunkle
Materie
63%

VOR 13,7 MILLIARDEN JAHREN
(Universum 380.000 Jahre alt)

Matter and energy portion of the universe today (above) and at the decoupling time (below), 380,000 years after the Big Bang. (Observations of the Wmapmission, etc) The term "atoms" stands for "normal matter".

1. In the book AstronSpaceOnomy we have proven that "dark matter" can be nothing more than a higher SPACE-energy-force concentration.
2. We assume that there is a maximum of energy and that it remains constant, albeit in different forms (matter, etc.).
3. Since the universe was still extremely concentrated shortly after the Big Bang, the SPACE energy was also extremely concentrated.
4. When matter (planets) moved here, at that time, it seemed, at 3-D observing, as it were barely moving.
5. The latter (4.), however, was only because we cannot "see" the energy waves of the SPACE concentration
6. So it was not the case that an unknown power hindered matter extremely (63%) in its movements, but

7. the matter, de facto, was moving extremely fast – as the SPACE wave distances (needed to measure the real speed) were extremely concentrated.

8. Today, the SPACE of universe is 50 billion lightyears in size. Space is no longer as concentrated as in the beginnings of universe. Matter (planets) can move more freely – and the mysterious "dark matter" has been reduced to 23% … (which we now reduced to 0%).

9. The SPACE waves distances have simply grown in size – and our arithmetic no longer needs to be left out of so much mystery.

In other words ...

a. ... the share of matter close to the Big Bang was 12% - and with it, the proportion of TIME power was relatively large.

b. Today, however, the proportion of matter is only 4.6%

c. Thus, the proportion of TIME is also falling congruently, while the SPACE share is increasing.

d. And with increasing SPACE content – at the universe borders and as well as VOIDs - the absorption power of the SPACE also grows.

e. During the big-bang, all dimensions of ENERGY were simply "just" driven outwards by the bang. The speed resulting from this primal bang for the matter parts would have been the normal expansion speed of the universe. The disproportionately strong force of the primal bang has outbid the potential forces of all sub-appearances (matter, gravity, space, time, ...) and initially hindered their effects and their possible influences.

f. But after that, SPACE was able to continuously build and expand its impact. And the further away the SPACE was from the primal bang and the materialistic realm of the universe, the stronger the SPACE became (up to matter--less VOIDs. And the stronger its sucking (VOIDs) power became. So while there was no "dark energy" at the big-bang, the proportion of "dark energy" today is 72% - and is nothing but the SPACE energy ($S = E$). SPACE is largely responsible for the hitherto unknown force that makes the universe grow faster than it "should".

F.3.3. The Relativity of TIME

F.3.3.1. The second: "s" - The measure of all times?

If energy and matter are relative according to Einstein, then TIME must also be relative, according to our TIME formula ($T = M / E$): A second is not a second everywhere. The – up to now "constant" unit measurement "second" is sometimes longer and sometimes shorter. Its duration depends to a large extent on the surroundings. The more matter, "m", and gravity, "g", determine the environment, the faster and more powerful the TIME force becomes. And thus, the shorter the life-time becomes, as "TIME" is destructive.

However, if you fly around a black hole at the speed of light, nothing can happen to you. One stays young because the direct environment (energy of the speed of light) counts more than the distant black-hole.

F.3.4. Double Relativity

The latter thoughts also lead to the fact that TIME also has to be relativized. This means that speed has to be considered twice relative: Under spatial- and time-relativity aspects.

Due to the concentration of space, the speed of light can now be faster than the "visible" speed of light (by "earthly" scales).

Due to the light wave extension tendency (light as such searches for more space, to achieve even faster speed), even more space waves passed per time-unit, if light thrives through a void. Because the actual measuring of time is based on speed through the "normal" vacuum of universe, "full" of neutrons (on average 1 per square-meter) … now, the invisible speed of light is increased again (we already increased it in combination with our discoveries behind "dark matter").

Additionally a double relativity has to be considered, as the TIME-waves expands (becomes less powerful). Thus, the time of a second "s" gets larger. And even more SPACE-waves can be surpassed in one second.

This increases the probability that even the earthly, Einsteinian "constant" "c²" can be achieved. It can be defined as a real(!) squared light speed(!!!). It does NOT have to be interpreted only as a constant(!), with which one was previously (before our inventions) only allowed to calculate the possible energy out of any matter. ☺

F.3.5. Visible versus invisible

3-dimensional-"space"-view versus non-visible-"SPACE"-view of the universe.

At this point we would like to question the dimensions of the universe calculated using today's methods. Both, the age of 13.8 billion years and the size of 50 billion light-years must be called into question here, because TIME and SPACE are relative. The results of age and size must be relativized with the relativities and correlations to/with the respective epochs.

A very special nuance of SPACE and TIME naturally comes down to its correlation. "Speed" as an "energetic dimension" should give us special information – and possibly also "standstill" (as zero speed).

Each of these sizes has already provided us with enormously efficient results and insights - also for our lives - through their extrapolation. But their combination will bring even greater results. Some combination results have already been hinted above, due to the correlations at that points. Deeper thoughts are following.

F.3.6. The SPACE-TIME-correlation

As the universe continues to "expand" the SPACE must become "bigger" or "stronger". SPACE gets the meaning of "(free)space" energy in the universe (is no longer primarily a 3-D view). The space power dwarfs everything else.

- The creation or granting of "energetic space" seems to be the most important thing in the universe. Humanity would be well advised to follow suit.

As the "speed" of "growth" increases, the break $(E/M)^2$ must be increasing
- This can only be done if E gets larger or/and M is getting smaller
- Since SPACE (E/M) and TIME (M/E) have reverse formulas, the space(power) gain must be at the expense of time(-power).
- SPACE and TIME correlate inversely proportionally – but overall the maximum potential energy is retained. At some places in universe with more matter – and at other places with less matter. Because SPACE and TIME consist of energy and matter, but they cannot increase the amount of potential maximum energy on their own.

  o This leads us to the following SPACE-TIME-CORRELATION:

✦ SPACE * TIME = 1
✦ $(E/M) * (M/E) = 1$ 😉

No matter, how much matter: the S-T-correlation keeps constant. But the surrounding will differ extremely, depending on the S- & T-values in detail!

F.3.6.1. Evidence concerning the SPACE-TIME-CORRELATION

- When (almost) all M converts into E, only SPACE remains
- When (almost) all E converts to M, there is (almost) only TIME left
- However, whether SPACE nor TIME can grow larger than E or M because they result from them – and therefore cannot directly affect E or M by themselves. They "only" result out of the combination of E and M at the corresponding places in universe.
- S or T can be maxima (e.g.: S = E), but never more than E.
- Since S and T cannot influence the E nor the M and cannot be "larger", the correlation between S and T can never be greater

than 1, (although both variables can be extremely large!). Otherwise there would be a potential influence. This "needed" result, "1" can (only) be achieved by multiplying space and time as a mutually depending correlation

✦ $(E/M) \times (M/E) = EM/ME = 1$!

Examples: S x T …
✦ $1 \times 1 = 1$ our „actual" universe
✦ $2 \times 0.5 = 1$ universe far away
✦ $0.25 \times 4 = 1$ universe close to gravitational concentrations

○ Through this correlation, the SPACE and TIME constellations in different universe areas can be taken into account without distorting the rest

○ This correlation may be surprising at first, but Isaac Newton had found a similar constancy for the forces of gravity and centrifugal force associated with matter

between the star and planets within the same structure (sun):
G + F = constant.***

> ✦ With Newton it is an addition, in our model it´s a multiplicative correlation of forces.

*** However, this correlation was not universal and was later refuted by Albert Einstein. As to Einstein, each planet finds its own orbit based on its energy constellations - in relation to that of the star. ****
**** According to our research, however, the truth of the orbits lies (also) in a SPACE- and TIME-energy-force-correlation between the star and the planets.

G. "SPEED"

The combination of SPACE and TIME as an increase in efficiency.

Above, we saw that new insights into increasing efficiency are already possible by purely extrapolating the dimensions SPACE and TIME.

Let us now turn to the more central dimension, which is composed of SPACE and TIME. This is defined from the earthly human perspective (initially) as "speed". However, this "speed" will lose its importance as a speed kit, in the course of reflection ... In favor of increasing efficiency.

In space, it is not primarily a question of speed, as is often suspected on Earth. Its more about increasing efficiency. We should therefore look for "general multipliers" on Earth as well, to improve our situation. Rather than focus primarily on "old fashioned" values, such as "speed" with its primarily material, spatial and temporal reference.

G.1. The "speed-paradox" - "earthly" vs. "astronomical" space & time formulas

G.1.1. Invisible "speed"
Time is relative, and as well space. This results out of a double-effect within "speed".

The space waves become shorter, more concentrated and stronger. Whereas the time waves become longer and weaker.

2 kilometers are squeezed down to 1 kilometer. This means: in 1 second we fly double as fast, if we consider the SPACE as power (being more present and therefore stronger) - and not as a "constant" 3-D-aspect. Additionally, time, 1 second, gets weaker, down to 0,5 seconds. Now the squeezed 2 kilometers can be passed in 0,5 seconds, instead of 1. That leads to 4 km in 1 sec, instead of 2 km in 1 sec. A double-effect towards speed.

If we leave our formula for "speed" "fixed" at the same constants (e.g.: kilometers per hour), then an object, for us, with our "view", at the edge of the universe, seams to continue to fly at the same speed as before, when flying closer to us. De facto, however, taking into account the real SPACE and TIME forces, this object flies many times faster.

We can't see SPACE- nor TIME-waves. However, we can see the implications of this:

G.1.2. Visible "non-speed increase" - violet light as optical illusion.

The more violet, the more an object appears to move away. That was a central discovery for the argument, that universe is expanding.

However, if the space waves appear more concentrated, then it just seems(!) as if this object is distancing from us. With increasing velocity, the stronger the light. Just because the color changes. But the color changes because the space is more concentrated. Because of the color, we reckon that the object has got farer and may be, become faster. De facto (with our measurement constants – if they would be able to be applied at that aspect) however, the object does not move (faster) away. But SPACE is getting stronger towards the outer edge of universe.

Through this kind of false conclusion (color), according to our measurement method, with constant meters, we calculate our universe larger than it is. The diameter of the universe, now calculated towards 50 billion light-years, must be smaller.

G.1.3. Secret "speed?"-"drivers". Void-bubbles and universe "all-round-outside-bubble"

There are huge bubbles (voids) between the galaxies and, as we suspect, also the bubble around our universe. According to our above mentioned findings, these are rapidly "growing" vacuum bubbles. These grow faster than the galaxies could do, as galaxies have cumbersome matter. The vacuum of these bubbles is so immense that it is able to drive the galaxies apart faster than they could ever do on their own, via the initial force from the big-bang or from solar winds via dust, initiating their birth

With these extremes in mind, we now want to question more precisely what "speed" is. What is this correlation from SPACE-(-route) per TIME(-clock).

At "speed" mankind immediately thinks of a car-(-tachometer) or mathematically primarily about the division of space by time. And at space primarily about chambers. And at time primarily about clocks. Everything is rather materially focused.

Universe thinks in broader dimensions ...

G.1.4. All-relative "speed"-formula

If we use universe-aspects for SPACE and TIME and now use these formulas of SPACE and TIME in the "human" formula for "speed" as "space" divided by "time", it turns out to:

$$\frac{E}{M} : \frac{M}{E} = \frac{E^2}{M^2} = \left(\frac{E}{M}\right)^2$$

One has not seen "speed" written this way, so far. Because mankind did not know the formulas of SPACE nor TIME. Therefore, mankind could not know their above-all correlation. It is a more general definition of "speed" – from the point of view of universe. Its more focused on general efficiency, rather than on "just" speed.

So far, we know for speed special dimensions, such as: "km/h" or "speed of light". However, these measurements are "earthly" definitions. Kilometers (km) or meters (m) have evolved as a fraction of the distance from the North Pole to the equator of the earth. Hours (h) have evolved from the earth's rotation, the time, which has been divided into 24 hours per rotation. And the speed of light is also measured in earthly (kilo-)-meters, although light is circulating throughout the universe.

However, if different SPACE concentrations and TIME forces in the universe are not taken into account, but our earthly units of measurement are still reckoned with, then there are precisely those misinterpretations. Misleading interpretations like i.a. the so called "dark matter": Why do the planets not circulate around their star faster than they should be able to do? Because of the gravity of an "unknown dark matter" was assumed …. In the book AstronSpaceOnomy[02] we were able to present this "dark matter" as a "thinking error".

Since SPACE is relative and TIME is relative, it is inevitable that speed must also be relative. With the above formula, we are transforming Albert Einstein's "fixed constant", the "c^2", into a variable, a relative force – without having to set ourselves to a fixed level. From now on, we always define speed as a correlation depending on local constellations.   And SPEED does not ultimately mean 3-D-speed, but may be "just" more SPACE (liberty) and less TIME (stress). Means: more astronomic efficiency !!!

G.1.5. The universe multiplier (-squaring ...)

Einstein's "c", "constant"-multiplicator corresponds to our space-time "speed" correlation "$(E/M)^2$" . But this is now a "variable" (instead of a "static") base multiplicator.

The "c^2", multiplier "constant" from Einstein's "simple relativity theory" then corresponds to "$(((E/M)^2))^2$ as a multiplier "variable", which leads to a 4-power-dimension $x^2 * x^2 = x^4$.

We have proven in AstronSpaceOnomy that the " c^2 " can also be seen as speed (and not as a constant, as up to the actual "status-quo").

With the above formula, we now prove that "SPEED" is relative, and can be an extremely powerful variable. It can do more than "only" speed or "only" calculate energy amounts. The exponent 4 is far stronger than Einstein's static contemplation in constellations close to earth and the solar system. And only here, in such similar systems, Einstein's formula functions "statically". In the rest of the universe, Einstein & Co's thoughts lead to "dark matter" and "dark energy" - while with our formulas everything seems pretty "Bright"... 😉

We not only explain the "darks". We not only regard the "now". To the Einstein´s & Co. "now" we now add the "past" and the "future". And we turn on new mathematical "lights" and insights towards the former dark. 😉

H. The new "Universal Dynamic(!) Relativity Formula"

However, the following must be taken into account:

From $E = m*c^2$ you can of course also calculate $E / m = c^2$. However, this E/m is something different from the E/M , which we have as a SPACE formula base.

- The E / m always calculates with constant kilometers per second.
- The E / M expects changing conditions of SPACE and TIME.
  - o Mankind has defined speed as space-unit per time-unit
  - o To briefly illustrate this, I merged our formula findings of S and T and determined $(E/M)^2$ as a formula for "relative speed" or more precisely: "efficiency".
- The dominance of SPACE in the universe shows that E/M has resulted to be SPACE and $(E/M)^2$ has resulted as EFFICIENCY. And efficiency considers the formulas of TIME and SPACE.
- This $(E/M)^2$ is the dynamic counterpart to Einstein´s "c". Our formulas for TIME and SPACE are just sub-forces within that "c",
  - o we just dynamized the "c"
    - o in the first step:
      - ✦ looking at it as velocity – and no longer as a constant.

105

- o in the second step
  - ✦ finding formulas for SPACE (as such) and TIME (as such)

With SPACE and TIME as sub-forces it is similar to the sub-forces of the "m" (within $E = m * c^2$): Where there is matter, there is GRAVITY and CENTRIFUGAL FORCE.

- In order to gain the "energetic force" (as the counterpart to " c^2 ") out of matter but now, with our(!) "efficiency formula", we rely on
  - o Albert Einstein´s 2nd power as verified, as it has resulted from many experiments on the part of Einstein.
  - o Our own definition of the "Simple Relativity" derived from other physic formulas.[02]
- I.e.: We square our pendant of Einstein´s "c" – and get: $(((E/M)^2))^2$.
  - o ATTENTION: For the sake of simplicity, we want to refer to $(E/M)^2$ as "z" in the future.

- We adopt the squaring as well for our "z", as the squaring is verified know-how to determine the possible maximum energy E out of any matter. It was verified by Einstein - and by us, using an alternative formula from physics, which "allowed" us, to use the "c" as "speed" – and no longer just as "constant" (as per Einstein).
- However, our "speed" base is different from Einstein's "c". The difference is as follows:
    - Einstein's "Simple Relativity Theory" ($E = m * c^2$) is static – and applies only to constellations similar to those in our solar system
    - Our "Simple Universal-Dynamic-Relativity-Theory"
      $$E = M * z^2$$

        - is dynamic (adapts to the respective correlations of SPACE-energy and TIME-energy)

- applies throughout the complete universe – i.e. also where, among other things, "dark matter" and "dark energy" are present,

- applies to the past and the future of universe aspects

H.1. The evidence of the "Universal Dynamic Relativity Theory"

Looking at the whole equation …

$$E = M * ((\,(E/M)^2\,))^2$$

… different constellations can take place:

H.1.1. The expansion limit: Voids and universe-limit at: $E = S$.

o Universe expansion: SPACE, E/M, grows, as E tends towards ∞ and M tends to zero;

✦ as long as M is > 0, a "powerful" (full of energy, not necessarily "big" in size) vacuum is created

✦ Energy kills matter. Either via the "power"(=energy) of a black-hole or via the "nothing-(inside-)tolerating" vacuum of a void. E, the counter of the SPACE-formula, tends to ∞ . And M, the nominator of SPACE tends to zero.

Already this increases the efficiency-multiplicator leading to explain far more of the up to now unknown energy forces, than Einstein could do with his formula. But considering that the 4th potency increases even more the counter and diminishes even more the nominator, leads to a tremendous multiplicator of the remaining M, with which the "z" is multiplied. This leads to explain even more % of the up to now not known energy forces. In the end: E = S is valid. An absolute vacuum is created – first as void, and last all the universe will be a vacuum... Energy equals SPACE

+ This efficiently generates the maximum of "energetic

space", "energy content" (not necessarily as a 3-D space).

+ This energetic "space" could be compared on Earth with the energy in our brains. The more intelligent humanity become, the more energy-charged will be the wealth, based on intelligent behavior (brain full of active, energetic connections). This then has little to do with the material orientation of much of today's humanity. But rather with empathy and transcendency. If all people were like that, we would have more prosperity.

+ But if all matter is gone, M = 0, everything ends in nothing-ness; a number divided by 0 is nothing. Nevertheless, this actually will not happen, since E is considered a maximum and constant(!) size. So, before M gets zero, there will be a relativization toward an equilibrium, however this might look like.

H.1.2. The matter rupture: super-nova = SPACE energy at E/M < 1

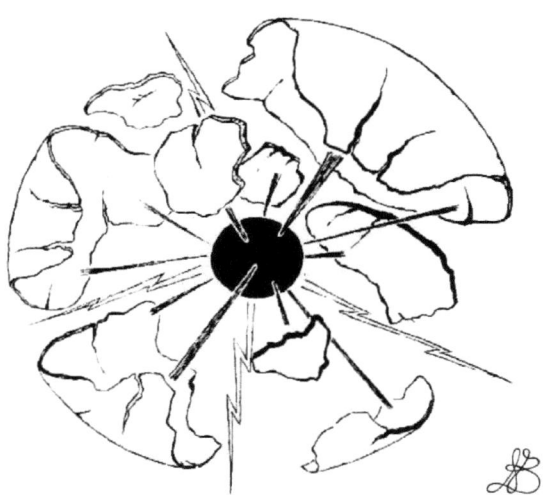

- Super-Nova: The multiplier, $(E/M)^4$ shrinks because M grows more than E. The E of the star "burns out", at the implosion. The remaining matter increases its relative power, due to over-proportional gravitation, coming from the concentrating (rest-)matter. The impact of a comet can also slow down the (energetic) rotation and thus take away part of the star "energy".

- As long as E/M>=1, the star is healthy
- As soon as E/M<1
  + i.a. … when E as equation result (left side of equation) shrinks, if matter gets lost by e.g. a super-nova or if the rotation becomes slower with the time going on
  + i.a. … when E in the counter (right side of equation) shrinks, as the original energy of stars shrinks via the continuous conversion of energy towards matter. This further aggravates the situation. A vicious circle begins …
  + … then it comes to the super-nova.

✦ Then, the E is "pressed" out
of the matter and M
disintegrates.

H.1.3. Rest matter rescue: Quasar

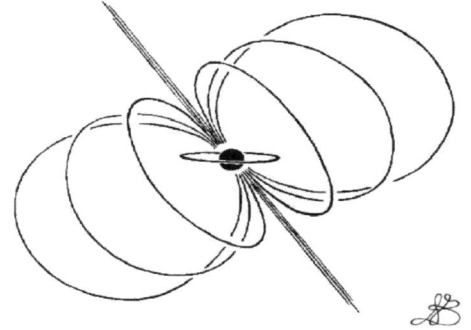

✦ As an intermediate stage of
matter decomposition at a
super-nova, possibly a
quasar remains.
✦ However, the matter
decomposition process
also continues with the
quasar as a vicious circle,
which also disintegrates the
rest

- ✦ Until E = 0, zero. M * 0/M is zero.
- ✦ With this E, however, only the energy from the star that got destroyed is meant. De facto no more energy can come from this star, hence the zero
- ✦ But all the energy from the ex-star has been made available to the rest of the universe – and this can grow with it.

H.1.4. Contraction limit: Black hole at E/M < 1

✦ Matter without (also: with too little) energy comes to e.g. a "standstill". So: …

- ○ … if the energy content of the star burns out - the E in the counter of the fraction of the right side of the equation tends to zero

- ○ … if the speed (orbit or/and rotation speed) decreases – then as well the E of our break E/M , our "z", our efficiency, becomes smaller – down to zero, at a standstill somewhen

✦ In both cases, the (energetic) efficiency multiplier gets down to (nearly) zero. But $E = M * 0$ would lead to no energy. But E must keep existing. So the only "energy" that may arise, when matter disappears due to lack of energy in its multiplicator is that of gravity (centrifugal force is no longer present in the above example. M had stored energy, but cant emit it any more, as M is dead).

- However, the energy of gravity is smaller than the original energy from matter with a full multiplier. So now we have to write:
  - $E_{(G)} = M$

- However, if a black-hole occurs, the energy loss of the multiplier does not occur successively, but extremely rapidly.
- The energy is not (all) released into the space to increase it, but is additionally concentrated in that already existing large gravitational force of a black-hole
- This great gravitational force has been accumulated more

and more in the course of a stellar growth and can "win" all the energy squeezed from the destroyed matter towards further gravitational force in a very large supernova ... and this vicious cycle ends in my formula from the book

Astronomic Solutions [09], where I relativized Einstein by extrapolating Newton´s gravity via the ideas of Einstein – and got the same amount of E, as Einstein discovered with his Simple Relativity:

$$\text{✦ } G=E\ ^{09}$$

- In doing so, the G – if it should become strong enough (as in black holes) also "kills" TIME, by destroying its base (the M, the matter).
- the strength of TIME which remained at the $M/E_{(G)}$-reststar has become relatively large - but when the gravitational

energy of a black hole is applied to this (small and energetically depleted) constellation of star- or planet-matter-rest (with hardly any residual energy - only $E_{(G)}$), then the last aspect of the matter of this planet/star also disintegrates... .

- Time dies with its planet or star. Time dies with the matter that is correlated with it. The planet or star disappears from space.

  - But gravity remains – at the other side of the equation. Gravity was always there, as a parallel force. But now, as the main force of SPACE efficiency has diminished or got lost, gravity takes over the dominating position. Gravity as to Newton[13] is:

$$F_1 = F_2 = G * \frac{m_1 + m_2}{r^2}$$

At a super-nova the r^2 turns towards zero. And - unless there is any matter rest at all – the division by a squared 0,0… figure and multiplication with the gravitational constant leads to a tremendous gravitation.

O Gravity concentrates in a black hole and also accumulates the residual energy, increasing the equation $G = E$ at both sides

O… which then again – with its gravity - "attracts" other planets, stars, etc. in order to repeat the destruction process with them as well.

O Stars and planets with too little energy (also as speed or rotation) are thus taken out of their orbit – and the universe is efficiently "cleaned".

O Unless there is some matter (planets etc., that can be absorbed) the black hole will continue to exist. But if all matter is gone – at least in the neighborhood – a zero results on the counter of the equation, leading the result, gravitation, to be zero – and to the disappearing of the black-hole.

O The rest of the universe now "wins" additional space.

I. EFFICIENCY

Efficiency is a central instruction for action in the universe. In Einstein's Simple Relativity Theory $E = m * c^2$ the importance of matter (m) is minimal. Central to the amount of energy (E) is the multiplier discovered by Einstein (c^2).

That this c^2 is more than a "constant" (with which the energy content of any kind of matter can be calculated). We have proven in the books AstronTimeOnomy[01] and AstronSpaceOnomy[02]. Here, in this book, AstronEfficiencyOnomy, we also prove the efficiency aspects of SPACE and TIME as such, as well as their correlation in combination. And by doing so, showing that this "efficiency" has far more value, than just "speed". We also succeeded in deriving the "c^2 " from another physical corner[02]. Now it is not primarily an extrapolation of many experiments from Einstein any longer. We, with the other formulas dynamized the " c " toward "velocity". Now we prove that energy and matter are also hidden in the c^2 . This leads to additional "efficiency" aspects. Each as part of "SPACE" and "TIME". We also prove the relativity of the SPACE and TIME formulas we found. And we described new ways of measuring our universe. No longer calculating space only as a constant, with meters. Nor determining time only as a constant, in seconds. We discovered so many aspects and orientations, that we have now renamed Einstein's c to z, so that it becomes clear that our equation wants more than just determining the energy out of matter. The universe wants more:

$$E = M * z^2$$

With this formula, the universe area that we focus on, primarily aims to gain one thing: "space energy". And this by means of efficient and sustainable use of existing materials and energies.

Mankind, on the other hand, seems to focus primarily on the material aspects. This wastes a lot of energy. A good example of this is that of the battery (matter) that is charged. You have to expend an extremely high amount of energy (E) to increase the size (matter) of the battery (by e.g. heating during charging) by only one millimeter. Most of the energy "crackles" in Einstein's "c^2". However, the "c^2" does not give any information about where most of the energy flows. According to our definition: the charging energy is needed for the "z" , i.e. the recharging of the emptied battery with "SPACE"-energy (!) and "TIME"energy (!) -aspects, that are hidden behind the "z". And, which are in direct correlation with the matter (battery acid), which is recharged, as they had been lost during the use of the battery. Only a very small part of the new energy goes into the matter enlargement of the battery. Mankind concentrates mostly just on the "large", matter. Universe focuses on the "z", efficiency.

The battery here is only symbolic. Symbolic for much investments in many things that do not necessarily have to be done. And the charging energy can also be optimized (instead of only taking into account regional material/ financial aspects): Instead of investing the "energy" and funds from/ for nuclear power plants or polluting coal-fired power plants and for nuclear fuel reprocessing and infinite/ unsafe nuclear waste storage. It is much cheaper and environmentally harmless to use solar energy. This could be extracted from a mini-area in the desert[10]:

Behind this picture there hide a lot of problems of our world…

At this point, I would like to refute only two main arguments:

"Every state wants to be autonomous in the supply of energy in order to be able to continue to exist in crises." One can only say:

1. This desert-point can also be distributed towards several points of the world, so that the dependence on only one area is reduced.
2. When the biggest looming crisis breaks out, no state needs any autonomy any

more – because when the environment dies, we all are dead.

"The desert project is not worth it, because 90% of the electricity is lost by cable-resistances on the way to the customers."

1. That is definitely wrong. Only 5% of the electricity is lost on the cable way.
2. Humanity is able to use and generate electricity more efficiently.
3. We have "system-problems". As to Albert Einstein "You can´t solve a problem with the same tools, which lead to it!". Let us relativize many "capital-rules" by topping our systems with "astronomy-rules".

The universe is many times more efficient. Why not copy some of the universe-rules for earthly purposes?

We urgently need a global wave of change.

We need the implementation of the ideas of www.world-wide-wealth.com which are detailed in the 3 books of the GlobalOnomy trilogy:

AstronTimeOnomy

AstronSpaceOnomy

AstronEfficiencyOnomy.

J. EFFICIENCY TRANSFER?!

Some differences and similarities between universe and mankind …

J.1. Principle aspects

J.1.1. Babies and common citizens

Babies around the world understand each other without problems – and without reservations.
And if we travel as ordinary citizens to foreign countries, we are (almost) welcome everywhere.

As well in space everything usually runs very peacefully (relatively speaking). There are only 1 to 2 super-nova every 100 years. Otherwise each planet and star go their own way without disturbing each other.

In our "world", on the other hand, so many companies and bubbles are "imploding", that after 100 years there remain only 1% of the companies listed in the Dow Jones 100 years before (USA study). There seems to be a problem with the systems(!) that the so-called "homo-sapiens" has imposed on the world.

J.1.2. Lyrics, Art & Music

Emotional aspects seems beautiful and unifying across borders.

Our emotional brain seems to be more "intel- ligent" or "objective", than the (in some ways- "educated") "rational" brain. This is because of the "rational" brain has been manipulated in the course of life and generations. It has been constrained in his way of "naturally" (see above) thinking. Fortunately, emotional- feeling is still present in many decision- making processes.
The universe also seems to love prettiness. In the visual painting of the effects from formulas, many drawings and patterns have "emerged" over time. They make the beauty and diversity of universe even more inte- resting than "only" the pictures and works of art of "just" the stars, galaxies or formulas. [11]

The formulas of the universe lead to efficiency and growth of the entire(!) universe. The formulas and systems of the so-called "homo-sapiens" have rather un-sustainable effects – at least for the vast majority of humanity. The homo-sapiens is not even able to manage the small world in a sustainable way. What a shame.

J.1.3. The brain - the fascinating computer

Technically, there are many parallels between the brain and the computer. Both are empty at the beginning. Both work with electric aspects. Many links can be made. Both have an enormous memory. And both, brain and PC (PCs, with "AI", artificial intelligence) come up with fascinating insights, time and again.

Purely "technically" (medically) there are also many parallels between brain and space. Those who learn, who challenge the brain, who look for more, and suck "knowledge energy" (for the vacuum), stay fit longer, get dementia less often. Sport makes the body fit, learning gets the brain fit.

Further up, we were able to demonstrate that in the universe SPACE is also energy, "SPACE energy" – and energy is primarily aimed at "increasing" the universal "SPACE". The brain also has SPACE energy without needing a lot of 3-D space. This SPACE energy increases as we "invest" "energy" in the brain. We need to educate children with more "SPACE", more liberty in – and curiosity for different - thinking. In the beginning we get emotional energy back: smile, laughter, developmental successes, ... Later that person can return more of this external energy back. Through his own ideas and activities. Even a computer can only provide results if it has been extensively produced and programmed with a lot of work (energy).

A human brain has between 100 billion and one trillion cells (depending on the counting considerations). Many of these cells have up to 10,000 connection-strings. These connect to other cells, so they can store and combine information. The memory is pretty much infinite. But: you have to want it and work for it in order to get the greatest possible benefit from your brain.

But: Those, who only want worker ants, prevent(!) training. This is not fair – but unfortunately it is everywhere. As well the type of training and programming can bring much mischief instead of usable results. And: there as well are "viruses" and "pirates" in the computer world. And those, who have been programmed or trained weakly or poorly, they easily fall victim to any crisis.

Yes, there are also "black holes" in the universe that destroy many "weak" planets or stars in their respective environments. But in the universe, the "weak" (not a good education, not enough money/base to go its own way) does not seem to be the primary goal. The universe promotes its own path for each planet – and has a solution for energetic enrichment for all(!).

J.1.3.1. The programming

The right "programing" of the brain is an essential aspect to become more efficient on earth:

- In the universe, SPACE and ENERGY prevail over MATTER (GRAVITATION) and TIME (at least at the part, we see).
- On Earth, matter and time prevail over space and energy through the industrial-capital-model-"embossing".

At "programming", it has to be considered that "efficiency" is something else everywhere on Earth ...

- Developed countries vs. developing countries
- Industry vs. service vs. agriculture – and all mentioned also vs. nature conservation
- State vs. companies vs. private vs. church
- Atheism vs. religion
- Christianity vs. Islam vs. Buddhism ...
- Catholics vs. Evangelists
- Dictatorship vs. communism vs. democracy vs. civil society
- Right vs. center vs. left
- Classics vs. neo-classics vs. Keynesians vs. monetarists vs. capitalists vs. "social" market economy, vs. plan-economy vs. laissez-faire

- fair competition vs. major bankruptcies vs. "too-big-to-fail" vs. "what-ever-it takes" over-indebtedness vs. "bad banks" vs. zero interest rate regulation vs. "quantitative easing" vs. inflation vs. speculative bubbles, machines vs. humans, ...

... all earthly think-models, "programming" – which do not exist in space, nor in the basic computer - and not in a purely technical (unprogrammed) area of the brain.

And all these opposites lead to blockages in thought, feeling and doing. And to conflicts instead of a coexistence (in space). One commits to something against something else - or "sees" things as "alternative-less" because no other solutions are there or are not seen (wanted or unwanted).

We need more (energetic) "space" in the brain, more links of cells, in order to be able to look at everything more openly and relatively, than many people can unfortunately see at present, due to too one-sided education.

And we all need more time. More time means: fighting against(!) time; Fight for more (free) space. More time for training – and more time before decisions or assessments. Also, in universe, there is the "rivalry" of TIME and SPACE. And as the SPACE-TIME-correlation $(S * T = 1)$ always yields 1, we need to fight for the SPACE and against the TIME. Those who are very much in (time) stress have no (free) space for "outside the box" perception of the environment. More freedom leads to more understanding, empathy and transcendence – and to a drastic reduction of the otherwise (wrongly) "programmed" conflicts.

The challenge: More time for the "we", the "us", the "our environment" (!). This depends on the "own" time - whereas this "own" time is a time-pattern, which is obstructed by the surrounding systems! And, time for others, today also means less one's own salary, less one's career, less (material) consumption, less profiling neurosis points, less the "I" of today's worldviews. The "I" today is very often not an inner "I", but a function (dependency) of the "environment". The environment forces us to do their needs. The state as the central star, organizing all the rest.

With this thinking we stand (astronomically) at the - long ago refuted (by Einstein) thoughts of Isaac Newton: The star (state) directs the planetary orbits (people's/ companies ...). Einstein discovered, that each planet/star optimizes its own orbit, with the energy received at birth.

To establish a similar system as Einstein´s finding on our Earth, we developed the LAZEB concept in the book AstronTimeOnomy[01].

As well towards universe, there have been a lot of different mankind thinking (see below). Let´s forget the past – and go new ways.

... The earth is flat and the center of the universe. All stars circle around the earth (Catholic Church)

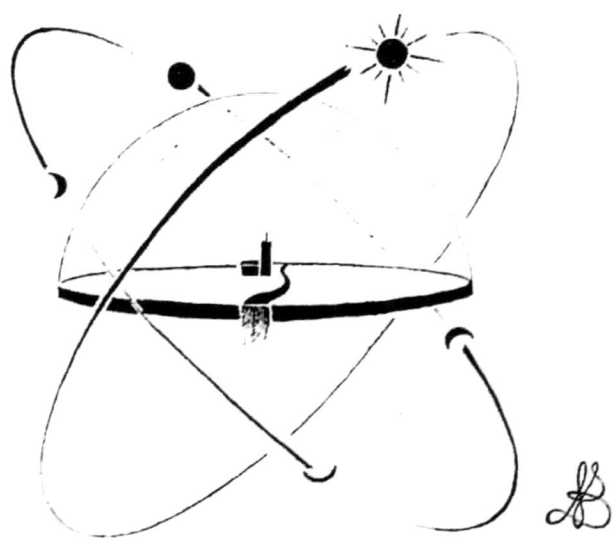

... The star determines the orbits of the planets (Isaak Newton)

... Each planet finds and optimizes its own path (Albert Einstein)

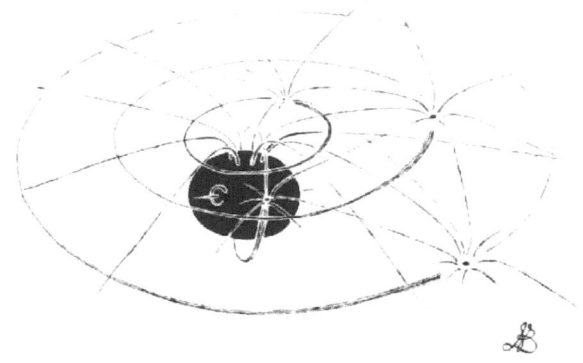

... The path optimization is done by means of SPACE-Energy(!) (Albert Bright) ...

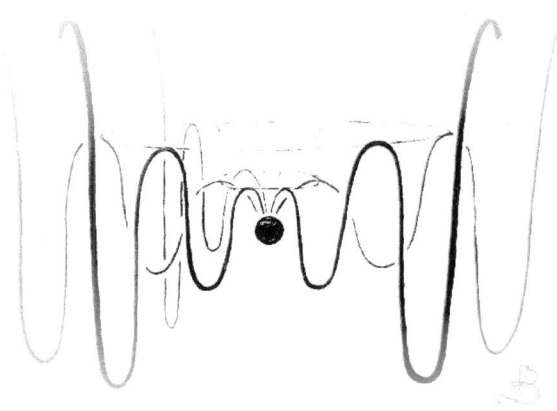

... in the fight against TIME energy(!) ...

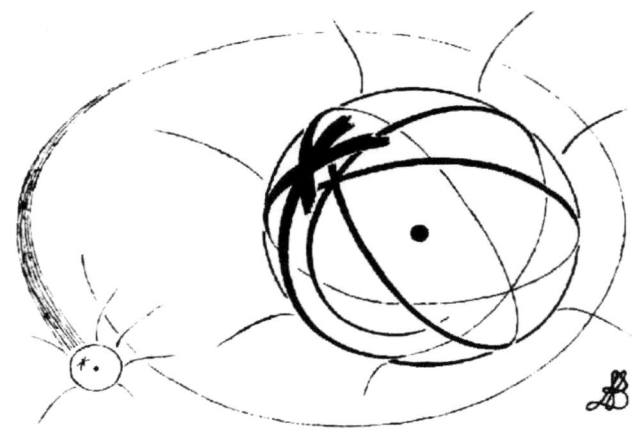

… and with a strong focus on efficiency…

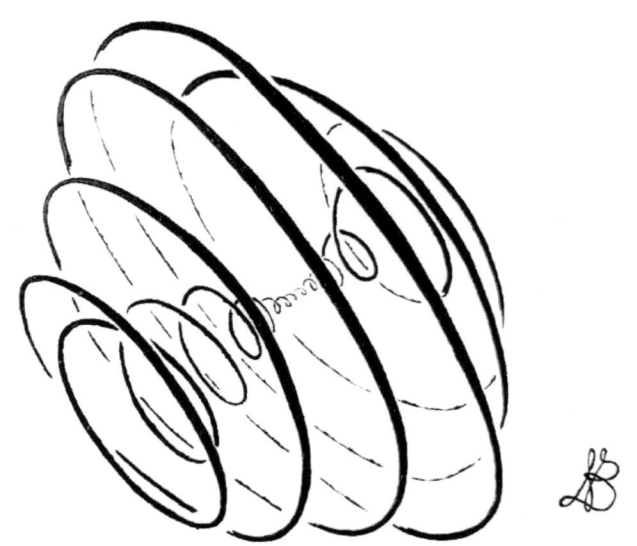

We now, want to reinforce these three last findings for humanity.

J.1.3.2. BIG-BANGS / IDEAS – and the surroundings

Real (!) innovations have always come from individuals who have had to fight against the respective establishment / environment / status-quo …

… either alone ("fight" for the "right" …)

- Galileo
- Columbus
- Einstein

... or with a group that has joined an idea (of initially a single one)

- French Revolution   Liberté, Égalité, Fraternité,
- Bourgeoisie vs. Nobility
- Olympia - all against all - and yet together - sporty.

Diversity is what really innovates ...

- Without knowledge base, no wisdom
- Without lateral thinking (from at least 2 sectors), less innovations
    o The brain is (technically) "open" to new connections of its cells
    o However, the human "establishment" is mostly (mentally) "closed"
        • why do we oppose the rules of our own brains?
        • Openness is what our brain (and space) wants. Openness is an essential efficiency multiplier! In many countries, this freedom even exists in the law: freedom of expression. However, this has not yet arrived in many brains and not at many decision-makers.

That is: Let´s get rid of all the barriers and blockages of thought – and we will become much more efficient. But this also means, among other things, more time for education and training.

J.1.3.3. Earthly/human aspects of SPACE and TIME

- SPACE versus space
    - According to our findings in the universe, SPACE has little to do with the importance, which we attach to "space" on earth.
    - SPACE is primarily energy - and hardly "material"
    - The "aspects" behind universal "SPACE" are transferable to earth rather as (energetic) aspects correlated to intelligence and knowledge in our brains, instead of any material stuff that we buy or areas that we conquer (warlike).

- SPACE is the greatest possible freedom in the universe - far from any material (compulsions).

⇨ If we want to live as effectively as the universe shows to us, we should ...
- begin to say goodbye to MATERIAL values as well as to the dictatorship of TIME,
- begin to focus more on "ENERGY values" (including knowledge, wisdom, transcendence) and indirect "SPACE values" (including freedom and peace).

⇨ TIME dictatorship and MATERIAL focus (as well, via gravity) are FLOPs, PATCHER.

⇨ Free SPACE and ENERGETIC expansion (via energy) are TOPs, PUSHER.

J.2. CHANCES

Purely emotional – and with an unbiased brain – the Earth could be prospering - for all humanity. If we succeed in removing the biggest barriers, many things can come "automatically". But the way to get there is a challenge – and is now being blocked once again by many crises and seemingly "insurmountable problems." System problems! These can hardly be overcome without system changes.

Leaving everything to the status quo will always lead to major crises and wars, time and again. True, the 17 UN Sustainable Development Goals are a good way to improve the world. But they still build too much on the "old". After all, all states have more or less agreed on them. And as such, it is a breakthrough that shows how urgently something "must be done" to eliminate poverty, disease, inequality, and many other abuses.

But, for example goal 1.: "No poverty", lamentably does not mean "achieving prosperity". And 5 years after start (2016) things got worse than before. And goal 16th: "peace" is far away from "freedom". And things in 2021 are worse than 2016. And many things still are interpreted differently by different countries. Two sides of one coin.

But all of them can be achieved with one measure: prosperity! With real prosperity. Without half-hearted models that continue to create dependence - e.g. salary or employment guarantees from the state, which would then only be feasible in rich states and would entail inevitable redistributive "fights", without knowing whether the redistributed funds would have more effect on the potential additional demand from the profiteers than they would have with the multiplier effects from which the money was taken …

With our models based on astronomy laws, we have shown in the last three books that things may run better. We will now be working for this in public.

We would like to welcome you as a prospect, sponsor or/and activist – at or for one of our two ways:

Prosperity & Sustainability:

 www.world-wide-wealth.com

Peace & Freedom:

 www.wise-star.org (not yet active)

K. THE ALTERNATIVE

Continue as before? That means:

The world will be destroyed!

.

ANNEX

01 Albert Bright, book: AstronTimeOnomy, ISBN 978-3-7526-0286-9, 1st GB-edition, 2021, (time formula).

02Albert Bright, book: AstronSpaceOnomy, ISBN 978-3-7534-4547-2, 1st GB-edition, 2021, (space formula).

03 DEFINITIONS (sorted alphabetically):

<u>Dark matter</u>: Why do Planets not orbit faster than they should be able to? x^{02}.

<u>Dark energy</u>: Why is the universe growing faster than calculable with actual parameter" (See this book).

<u>Refraction</u> via TIME & SPACE forces - see x^{02}

<u>space</u>	Written in small letters means: in 3-D-space.
<u>SPACE</u>	For the SPACE formula, see x^{02} energy-concentration vs. space curvature. See x^{02}, Chapter B.8.3.
<u>TIME</u>	Written in capital means: in our formula it is a force, instead of seconds or hours etc.
	For the TIME formula, see x^{01}

04 ACCORDING to our findings, SPACE and TIME are variable – and relative! SPACE is not always equal to the 1 meter defined by humans (a 10-millionth part of the distance from the North Pole to the equator – or a correlation with the speed of light). And TIME is not the same everywhere with the second, which has arisen from the evolution of the earth.

05 "The human mind treats a new idea the same way the body treats a strange protein, it rejects it." (Peter Medawar, "economist", 02-10-2019)

06 "If they were right, one would have been enough!" Albert Einstein in response to the "Association of Astronomers Against the Theories of Einstein" founded by 100 astronomers against him - according to Stephen Hawking, book: A Briefer History of Time, 2008.

07 Johann Wolfgang von Goethe: Actually, you only know, when you know little. With knowledge, doubt grows. Maxims and Reflections, From Art and Antiquity, 1826.

[08] Stephen Hawking and Leonard Mlodinow, A Briefer History of Time, 2008.

[09] Albert Bright, Astronomic Solutions, British Library, 2014, ISBN 978-0-9930836-0-0, p. 34 ff.

[10] Image from "Catapult Magazine"

[11] Visit our virtual gallery on www.world-wide-wealth.com where some exhibits are displayed – or make an appointment for our real gallery.

[12] The composition of Universe:

(A.) now & past

1st Today (72% dark energy); 2nd 13.7 billion years ago (63% dark matter) …

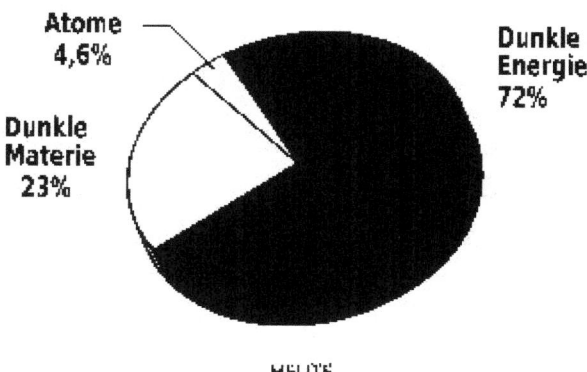

HEUTE

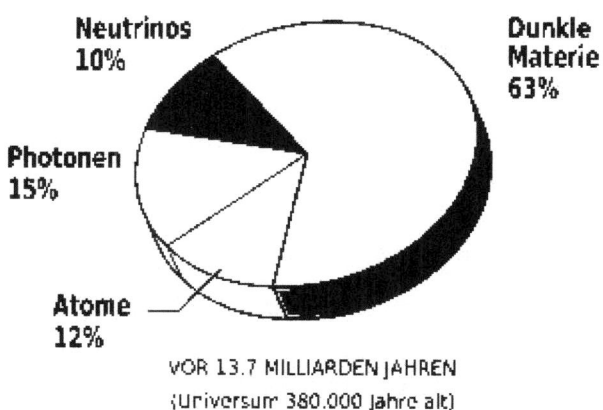

VOR 13.7 MILLIARDEN JAHREN
(Universum 380.000 Jahre alt)

Graphics and infos from "Wikipedia":

Matter and energy portion of the universe at present (above) - and (below), 380,000 years after the big bang. (Observations of the WAMP-Mission and others.).[1] The term "atoms" stands for "normal matter".

149

(B.) Tomorrow:

100% SPACE-Energy

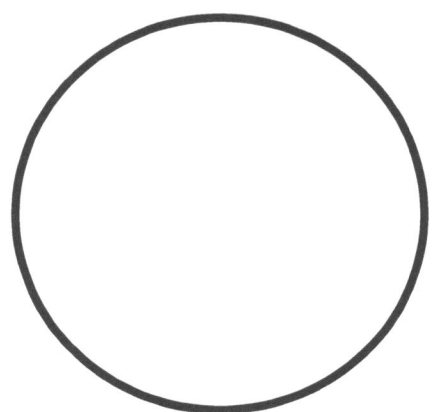

[13] It is easier to calculate and show things with Newtons gravity, rather than with Einstein´s gravity. AND: mankind still lands on the Mars with Newton … although, yes, electronic navigation on earth would not be perfect, without Einstein …

Notes:

.